Anna Hazare

Return of the Mahatma

Some Quotes of Anna Hazare

"Ban on consumption and sale of alcohol lays the foundation of rural development."

"It is impossible to change the village without transforming the individual. Similarly it is impossible to transform the country without changing its villages."

"In the process of rural development, social and economic development should go hand in hand."

"The ultimate goal of all politics and social work should be the upliftment of society and of the nation."

"Books alone cannot prepare future citizens, it requires cultural inputs to do so."

"Educational institutions are not enough to make good citizens, every home should become an educational center."

"One should not accept anything free; accepting charity makes one lazy and dependent."

"One who performs all worldly functions and still remains detached from worldly things is a true saint."

"It is experience that gives the direction but it is youth that gives the drive to every plan."

Anna Hazare

Return of the Mahatma

Kaushal Goyal

Author of

Barack Obama: Dreams Come True

Pigeon Books India
New Delhi, India.

ANNA HAZARE

RETURN OF THE MAHATMA

First Edition, September 2011

DISCLAIMER

The contents and material for this book is collected from the internet, newspapers, magazines, books and various other sources. As the book is based on the actual happenings and life of Anna Hazare, it is not possible to list all the sources of information.

Please see 'Selected Bibliography' on page no.179 for major internet search engines, websites, newspapers, magazines and books from which the editor has taken material for the book.
The editor has not added any matter and taken complete care and precautions in compilation.

The publishers & editor have tried their best to ensure that the text is authentic and correct upto September, 2011. They are in no way to be held responsible for any part, opinions and views expressed in this book.

ISBN: 978-8188951-70-3

Published by

Pigeon Books India

An Imprint of

gbd books

I-2/16, Ansari Road, Daryaganj,
New Delhi - 110002, India.
generalbookdepot@yahoo.com
www.goyalbookshop.com
Ph.: 9810229648, 9312286851

Printed at
Radha Press, Delhi - 110031
radha.press@yahoo.co.in

Contents

Anna Hazare: Return of the Mahatma

"My Dear Countrymen, the second freedom struggle has begun. I have been arrested as well. Will this struggle stop with my arrest? Absolutely not. You should not let that happen. The entire world has come to know how deep rooted corruption is."

—Anna Hazare

1
Kisan Baburao Hazare

"The gap between the rich and poor is increasing. Some are living to eat, while others are struggling to eat enough to be able to live."

–Anna Hazare

Kisan Baburao Hazare, popularly known as Anna Hazare is an Indian social activist who is recognised for his participation in the 2011 Indian anti-corruption movement. Hazare also contributed to the development and structuring of Ralegan Siddhi, a village in Parner taluka of Ahmednagar district, Maharashtra, India. He was awarded the Padma Bhushan, the third-highest civilian award–by the Government of India in 1992 for his efforts in establishing this village as a model for others.

From a tenacious soldier to a social reformer, and a right to information crusader, Anna Hazare's journey of four decades has been unprecedented in terms of a non-violent yet effective campaign of resurrecting a barren village into an `ideal village' model and empowering the faceless citizen through pioneering work on Right to Information. His efforts to empower *grampanchayats*, protect efficient government officers from frequent transfers and fight against the red tapism in government offices have also received accolades.

Anna Hazare started a hunger strike on 5 April 2011 to exert pressure on the Indian government to enact a strict anti-corruption law as envisaged in the Jan Lokpal Bill, for the institution of an ombudsman with the power to deal with corruption in public offices. The fast led to nation-wide protests in support of Hazare. The fast ended on 9 April 2011, the day after the government accepted Hazare's demands. The government issued a gazette notification on the formation of a joint committee, constituted of government and civil society representatives, to draft the legislation.

Anna has been featured as the most influential person in Mumbai by a national daily newspaper.He has faced criticism by political commentators for his authoritarian views on justice, including death as punishment for corrupt public officials and support for forced vasectomies as a method of family planning.

EARLY LIFE

Kisan Hazare was born on 15 June 1937 in Bhingar, a small village near the city of Hinganghat, in Bombay Province (present-day Maharashtra). Kisan's father, Baburao Hazare, worked as an unskilled labourer in Ayurveda Ashram Pharmacy. Kisan's grandfather was working for the army in Bhingar, when he was born. The grandfather died in 1945, but Baburao continued to stay at Bhingar. In 1952, Baburao resigned from his job and returned to his own village, Ralegan Siddhi. Kisan had six younger siblings and the family faced significant hardships. Kisan's childless aunt offered to look after him and his education, and took him to Mumbai. Kisan studied up to the seventh standard in Mumbai and then sought employment, due to the economic situation in his household. He started selling flowers at Dadar to support his family. He soon started his own shop and brought two of his brothers to Bombay.

MILITARY SERVICE

His tryst with the army came when many Indian soldiers became martyrs in the Indo-China War of 1962 and the Government of India had appealed to young Indians to join the Indian army. Being passionate about patriotism, he promptly responded to the appeal and joined the Indian Army in 1963. Despite not meeting the physical requirements, 25-year-old Hazare was selected, as emergency recruitment was taking place in the Indian Army. During his 15-year tenure as a soldier, he was posted to several states like Sikkim, Bhutan, Jammu-Kashmir, Assam, Mizoram, Leh and Ladakh and braved challenging weathers. After training at Aurangabad in Maharashtra he started his career in the Indian Army as a driver in 1963. During the Indo-Pakistani War of 1965, Hazare was posted at the border in the Khem Karan sector. On 12 November 1965, Pakistan launched air attacks on Indian bases, and all of Hazare's comrades were killed; he was the only survivor of that convoy. It was a close shave for Hazare as one bullet had passed by his head. He was driving a truck. This led him

to dwell on the purpose and meaning of life and death. At times, Hazare used to be frustrated with life and wondered about the very existence of human life. His mind yearned to look out for a solution to this simple and basic question. His frustration reached the peak level and at one particular moment, he also contemplated suicide. For this, he had also penned a two page essay on why he wants to live no more. Fortunately for him, inspiration came from the most unexpected quarters–at the book stall of the railway station of New Delhi, where he was located then. He came across a book of Swami Vivekananda "Call to the youth for nation building" and immediately bought it.

He was inspired by Vivekananda's photograph on the cover. As he started reading the book, he found answers to all his questions, he says. The book revealed to him that the ultimate motive of human life should be service to humanity. Striving for the betterment of common people is equivalent to offering a prayer to the God, he realized. He realized that saints sacrificed their own happiness for that of others, and that he needed to work towards ameliorating the sufferings of the poor. He started to spend his spare time reading the works of Vivekananda, Gandhi, and Vinoba Bhave. During the mid-1970s, he again survived a road accident while driving. He decided not to let go of a life-time by being involved merely in earning the daily bread for the family. That's the reason why he pledged to be a bachelor. By then he had completed only three years in the army and so would not be eligible for the pension scheme. In order to be self-sufficient, he continued to be in the army for 12 more years. After that, he opted for voluntary retirement and returned to his native place in Ralegan Siddhi, in the Parner Tehsil of Ahmednagar district. It was at that particular moment that Hazare took an oath to dedicate his life to the service of humanity, at the age of 38. He took voluntary retirement from the army in 1978.

In the Army five medals were notified to Anna Hazare–

1. Sainya Seva Medal,
2. Nine Years Long Service Medal,
3. Sangram Medal,
4. 25th Independent Anniversary Medal
5. Paschimi Star

2

TRANSFORMATION OF RALEGAN SIDDHI

"The dream of India as a strong nation will not be realized without self-reliant, self-sufficient villages, this can be achieved only through social commitment and involvement of the common man."

–Anna Hazare

While in the army, Hazare used to visit Ralegan Siddhi for two months every year and used to see the miserable condition of farmers due to water scarcity. Ralegan Siddhi falls in the drought-prone area with a mere 400 to 500 mm of annual rainfall. There were no weirs to retain rainwater. During the month of April and May, water tankers were the only means of drinking water. Almost 80 per cent of the villagers were dependent on other villages for food

grains. Residents used to walk for more than four to six kilometers in search of work and some of them had opted to open country liquor dens as a source of income.

More than 30-35 such dens located in and around the village had tarnished the dignity of the village and marred the social peace. Small scuffles, thefts and physical brawls resulted in loss of civic sense. Morality had reached such a nadir that some of the residents stole wooden logs of the temple of the village deity Yadavbaba to burn the choolah of one of the country liquor outfits.

Hazare came across the work of one Vilasrao Salunke, a resident of Saswad near Pune who had started a novel project of water management through watershed development in a joint venture with the *Gram Panchayat*. Hazare visited the project and decided to implement it in Ralegan Siddhi. By keeping an eye on conserving every drop of water and preventing erosion of the fertile soil, he steered the villagers to begin working towards water conservation. At the outset, they completed 48 Nala Bunding work, contour trenches, staggered trenches, gully plugs, meadows development and of forestation of 500 hectares of land. Thereafter, they constructed five RCC weirs and 16 Gabion Weirs.

This resulted in increase in the ground water level. After that, Hazare along with his team worked out the cropping pattern suitable to the quality of soil and the water volume available for farming. This led to increase in the water table by making water available for 1,500 acres of land instead of 300 acres. As a natural sequel, this effort led to yielding of food-grains and the villagers became self-sufficient in terms of food. The table turned turtle–earlier there was no work available for the villagers, now manpower was required to be imported from neighbouring villages.

The changes in the economics brought all the villagers under one roof of unity and people voluntarily contributed in terms of labour and money to build a school, a hostel, a temple and other buildings. Mass marriages, grains bank, dairy, cooperative society, self-help groups for women and youth mandals helped develop the village in all aspects and gave a new face to it.

Hazare opines that proper planning of natural and human resources can result in the betterment of a person, area, village instead of exploiting such resources. He says,

"Today we all are exploiting the earthen resources like petrol, diesel, kerosene, coal and water. This can never be termed as perennial development as it is going to lead a state of destruction one day. The sources of energy are limited and hence I am concerned about the next generations. Today many of the villages of almost every state are feeling the brunt of water shortage. Building concrete jungles does not mean development as Gandhiji had rightly said.

Creation of a human idol should be the main objective rather than creating towering buildings. Surely, one needs to live for oneself and the family but simultaneously one owes something to your neighbour, your village and your nation too. For this, you need an idol who could lead to this goal. Such leadership is not created by power or money but only by virtues like pure thinking, matching action and willingness to sacrifice. It is the thumb rule of farming that – When a seed buries itself, it leads to a better yield. in order to get better yield of grains, one single grain needs to burry itself.

The society needs such volunteers who are ready to get buried in selfless service for the better future of the society."

–Anna Hazare

Hazare's Ralegan Siddhi became the first role model of an ideal village and has become a tourist spot for many visitors across the nation, since it shows the metamorphoses from the worst village to an ideal village. Visitors include politicians, researchers, social workers and students. Four postgraduate students have completed Ph. D. thesis on Ralegan Siddhi.

PROHIBITION ON ALCOHOL

Anna Hazare recognised that without addressing the menace of alcoholism, no effective and sustainable reform was possible in the village. He organised the youth of the village into an organisation named the *Tarun Mandal* (Youth Association). Hazare and the youth group decided to take up the issue of alcoholism. At a meeting conducted in the temple, the villagers resolved to close down liquor dens and ban alcohol in the village. Since these resolutions were made in the temple, they became in a sense religious commitments. Over thirty liquor brewing units were closed by their owners voluntarily. Those who did not succumb to social pressure were forced to close down their businesses when the youth group smashed up their liquor dens. The owners could not complain as their businesses were illegal.

When some villagers were found to be drunk they were tied to poles/pillars of the temple and flogged, sometimes personally by Hazare. He justified this harsh punishment by stating in an interview to Reader's Digest in 1986 that "rural India was a harsh society".

Hazare said, "Doesn't a mother administer bitter medicines to a sick child when she knows that the medicine can cure her child? The child may not like the medicine, but the mother does it only because she cares for the child. The alcoholics were punished so that their families would not be destroyed."

Hazare appealed to the government of Maharashtra to bring in a law whereby prohibition would come into force in a village if 25% of the women in the village demanded it. In July 2009 the state government issued a government resolution amending the Bombay Prohibition Act, 1949. As per the amendments, if at least 25% of women voters demand liquor prohibition through a written application to the state excise department, voting should be conducted through a secret ballot. If 50% of the voters vote against the sale of liquor, prohibition should be imposed in the village and the sale of liquor should be stopped. Similar action can be taken at the ward level in municipal areas. Another circular was issued making it mandatory to get the sanction of the *Gram Sabha* (the local self-government) for issuing new permits for the sale of liquor. In some instances, when women agitated against the sale of liquor, cases were filed against them. Hazare took up the issue again. In August 2009 the government issued another circular that sought withdrawal of cases against women who sought prohibition of liquor in their villages.

It was decided to ban the sale of tobacco, cigarettes, and *beedies* (an unfiltered cigarette where the tobacco is rolled in tendu also known as Diospyros Melanoxylon leaves instead of paper) in the village. In order to implement this resolution, the youth group performed a unique "Holi" ceremony. The festival of Holi is celebrated as a symbolic burning of evil. The youth group brought all the tobacco, cigarettes, and *beedies* from the shops in the village and burnt them in a 'Holi' fire. Tobacco, cigarettes, or beedies are no longer sold in Ralegan Siddhi.

GRAIN BANK

In 1980, the Grain Bank was started by him at the temple, with the objective of providing food security to needful farmers during times of drought or crop failure. Rich farmers, or those with surplus grain production, could donate a quintal to the bank. In times of need, farmers could borrow the grain, but they had to return the same amount of grain they borrowed, plus an additional quintal as an interest. This ensured that nobody in the village ever went hungry or had to borrow money to buy grain. This also prevented distress sales of grain at lower prices at harvest time.

WATERSHED DEVELOPMENT PROGRAMME

> *"It is not the water in the fields that brings true development, rather, it is water in the eyes, or compassion for fellow beings, that brings about real development."*
>
> *–Anna Hazare*

Ralegan is located in the foothills, so Hazare persuaded villagers to construct a watershed embankment to stop water and allow it to percolate and increase the ground water level and improve irrigation in the area. Residents of the village used *shramdan* (voluntary labour) to build canals, small-scale check-dams, and percolation tanks in the nearby hills for watershed development. These efforts solved the problem of water scarcity in the village and made irrigation possible. The first embankment that was built using volunteer efforts developed a leak and had to be reconstructed, this time with government funding.

In order to conserve soil and water by checking runoff, contour trenches and gully plugs were constructed along the hill slopes. Grass, shrubs and about 3 Lakh (300,000) trees were planted along the hillside and the village. This process was supplemented by afforestation, *nullah bunds*, underground check dams, and cemented *bandharas* (small diversion weirs) at strategic locations. Ralegan has also experimented with drip and bi-valve irrigation. Papaya, lemon, and chillies have been planted on a plot of 80 acres (32 ha) entirely irrigated by the drip irrigation system. Cultivation of water-intensive crops like sugar cane was banned. Crops such as pulses, oil-seeds, and certain cash crops with low water requirements were grown. The farmers started growing high-yield varieties of crop and the cropping pattern of the village was changed. Hazare has helped farmers of more than 70 villages in drought-prone regions in the state of Maharashtra since 1975. When Hazare came in Ralegan Siddhi in 1975 only 70 acres (28 ha) of land was irrigated, Hazare converted it into about 2,500 acres (1,000 ha).

The Government of India plans to start a training centre in Ralegan Siddhi to understand and implement Hazare's watershed development model in other villages in the country.

MILK PRODUCTION

As a secondary occupation, milk production was promoted in Ralegan Siddhi. Purchase of new cattle and improvement of the existing breed with the help of artificial insemination and timely guidance and assistance by a veterinarian resulted in an improvement in the cattle stock. Milk production has increased. Crossbreed cows are replacing local ones which gave a lower milk yield. The number of milk cattle has also been growing, which resulted in growth from 100 litres (before 1975) to around 2,500 litres per day. The milk is sent to a co-operative dairy (Malganga Dairy) in Ahmednagar. Some milk is given to *Balwadi* (kindergarten) children and neighbouring villages under the child nutrition program sponsored by the *Zilla Parishad.*

From the surplus funds generated, the milk society bought a mini-truck and a thresher. The mini-truck is used to transport milk to Ahmednagar and to take vegetables and other produce directly to the market, thus eliminating intermediate agents. The thresher is rented out to farmers during the harvesting season.

EDUCATION

In 1932, Ralegan Siddhi got its first formal school, a single classroom primary school. In 1962, the villagers added more classrooms through community volunteer efforts. By 1971, out of an estimated population of 1,209, only 30.43% were literate (72 women and 290 men). Boys moved to the nearby towns of Shirur and Parner to pursue higher education, but due to socio-economic conditions, girls could not do the same and were limited to primary education. Hazare, along with the youth of Ralegan Siddhi, worked to increase literacy rates and education levels. In

1976 they started a pre-school and a high school in 1979. The villagers formed a charitable trust, the *Sant Yadavbaba Shikshan Prasarak Mandal*, which was registered in 1979.

The trust obtained a government grant of Indian ₹ 400,000 (US$8,920) for the school building using the National Rural Education Programme. This money funded a new school building that was built over the next two months using volunteer labour. A new hostel was constructed to house 200 students from poorer sections of society. After the opening of the school, a girl from Ralegan Siddhi became the first female in the village to complete her Secondary School Certificate in 1982. Since then the school has been instrumental in bringing in many of changes to the village. Traditional farming practices are taught in this school in addition to the government curriculum.

REMOVAL OF UNTOUCHABILITY

The social barriers and discrimination that existed due to the caste system in India have been largely eliminated by Ralegan Siddhi villagers. It was Anna Hazares moral leadership that motivated and inspired the people of Ralegan Siddhi to shun untouchability and discrimination against the Dalits. People of all castes come together to celebrate social events. Marriages of Dalits are held as part of community marriage program together with those of other castes. The Dalits have been integrated into the social and economic life of the village. The upper caste villagers have built houses for the lower caste Dalits by Shramdaan, Sanskrit for voluntary work without payment, and helped to repay their loans to free them from their indebtedness.

COLLECTIVE MARRIAGES

Most rural poor get into a debt trap as they incur heavy expenses at the time of marriage of their daughter or son. It is an undesirable practice but has almost become a social obligation in India. Ralegan's people have started celebrating marriages collectively. Joint feasts are held, where the expenses are further reduced by the *Tarun Mandal* taking responsibility for cooking and serving the food. The vessels, the loudspeaker system, the mandap, and the decorations have also been bought by the Tarun Mandal members belonging to the oppressed castes. From 1976 to 1986, 424 marriages have been held under this system.

GRAM SABHA

The Gandhian philosophy on rural development considers the *Gram Sabha* as an important democratic institution for collective decision making in the villages of India. Hazare campaigned between 1998 and 2006 for amending the *Gram Sabha* Act, so that the villagers have a say in the development works in their village. The state government initially refused, but eventually gave in due to public pressure. As per the amendments, it is mandatory to seek the sanction of the *Gram Sabha* (an assembly of all village adults, and not just the few elected representatives in the gram panchayat) for expenditures on development works in the village. In case of expenditure without the sanction of the *Gram Sabha*, 20% of *Gram Sabha* members can lodge a complaint to the chief executive officer of the *zilla parishad* (the district-level governing body) with their signatures. The chief executive officer is required to visit the village and conduct an inquiry within 30 days and submit a report to the divisional commissioner, who has the power to remove the sarpanch or deputy sarpanch and dismiss the gram sevak involved. Hazare was not satisfied as the amended Act did not include the right to recall a sarpanch. He insisted that this should be included and the state government relented.

In Ralegan Siddhi, *Gram Sabha* meetings are held periodically to discuss issues relating to the welfare of the village. Projects like watershed development activities are undertaken only after they are discussed in the *Gram Sabha*. All decisions like *Nashabandi* (bans on alcohol), *Kurhadbandi* (bans on tree felling), *Charai bandi* (bans on grazing), and *Shramdan* were taken in the *Gram Sabha*. Decisions are taken in a simple majority consensus. The decision of the *Gram Sabha* is accepted as final.

In addition to the panchayat, there are several registered societies that take care of various projects and activities of the village. Each society presents an annual report and statement of accounts in the *Gram Sabha*. *The Sant Yadavbaba Shikshan Prasarak Mandal* monitors the educational activities. The *Vividh Karyakari Society* gives assistance and provides guidance to farmers regarding fertilizers, seeds, organic farming, and financial assistance. The *Sri Sant Yadavbaba Doodh Utpadhak Sahakari* Sanstha gives guidance regarding the dairy business. Seven co-operative irrigation societies provide water to the farmers from cooperative wells. The *Mahila Sarvage Utkarsh Mandal* attends to the welfare needs of women.

3

Social Life of Anna Hazare

"Anna is a shining example of creativity and service by an ex-Serviceman."

–Field Marshal K.M. Cariappa *(in 1991)*

Anna rightly thought that Development is marred by corruption and started a new venture in 1991 called *Bhrashtachar Virodhi Jan Aandolan* (BVJA) or public movement against corruption. It was found that some 42 forest officers had duped the state government for crores of rupees through corruption in confederacy. Hazare submitted the evidences to the government but the latter was reluctant to take action against all these officers as one

of the ministers of the ruling party was involved in the scam. A distressed Hazare returned the Padmashree Award to the President of India and also returned the Vriksha Mitra Award given by then Prime Minister of India Rajiv Gandhi.

He further went on an indefinite hunger strike in Alandi on the same issue. Finally, the government woke up from deep slumber and took action against the culprits. Hazare's sustained campaign on this issue had a great effect –six of the ministers were forced to resign and more than 400 officers from different government offices were sent back to home.

Hazare realized that it was not enough to merely take action against fraudulent ministers or officers but to change the entire system that was studded with loopholes. Hence, he campaigned for the Right to Information Act. The state government turned a blind eye towards the pleas in this regard and so he first agitated in the historical Azad Maidan in Mumbai in the year 1997. To create mass public awareness about RTI amongst the youth, Hazare traveled extensively throughout the state. The government kept promising that RTI Act would be made but never raised this issue in the house or the state assembly. Hazare did not relent–he agitated at least ten times.

Finally, again he went on an indefinite hunger strike at Azad Maidan in the last week of July 2003. At last, the President of India signed the draft of the Right to Information Act after his 12-day-long hunger strike and ordered the state government to implement it with effect from 2002. The same draft was considered as the base document for the making of the National Right to Information Act-2005.

After the implementation of the RTI Act-2005, Hazare travelled for more than 12,000 Kms across the state creating awareness about the Act. In the second phase, he interacted with more than one lakh college students and also conducted mass public meetings across 24 districts of the state. The third phase included daily 2-3 public meetings in more than 155 tehsil places. In this massive campaign, posters, banners were displayed and more than one lakh booklets of the provisions of the Act were distributed at a nominal price.

This created enough of awareness and people were educated on the issue of rights of citizens.

Hazare deservedly won the coveted Padmashree and then Padmabhushan. Care International of the USA, Transparency International, Seoul (South Korea) also felicitated him. Apart from this, he received awards worth Rs 25 lakh and donated the entire amount for the Swami Vivekananda Kritadnyata Nidhi (social gratitude fund). Out of the two lakh rupees received from the above amount, mass marriages are carried of at least 25-30 poor couples every year.

That Hazare has given his life for social betterment is reflected thus: "I do have my home in the village but I have not entered it for the past 35 years. I have implemented schemes costing more than several crores of rupees but I do not have bank balance. Last 12 years I have been working in the field of eradication of corruption. This movement is run entirely by public support without and grants or sponsorships. I appeal for money wherever I go for a public meeting and urge them to contribute generously. The same money I use to carry out my campaigns. The money collected at such public meetings is counted in front of the villagers and my volunteers issue a receipt of the same on the spot."

He further states that, "The movement that we started many years back without a penny in wallet, has spread its wings in all the 33 districts and 252 tehsils of the state. Hence we have been instrumental in offering rights to local bodies like *Gramsabha*, preventing red-tapism and initiating the law of transfers. This has prevented corruption on a large scale. This has also resulted in offering social justice to the economically backward class. The Union Government

keeps on making various schemes for poor people in availing kerosene, LPG and pulses on ration card but the middlemen keep on gulping the subsidies of the same. Our efforts made these necessities available to the poor."

The state government promoted opening of cooperative societies, credit societies & urban banks. Believing in the principles of cooperative sector, the utmost lower class of the society invested their savings with such cooperative societies. However, the directors of such societies devoured the money and failed to pay back the basic amount to the members of the societies. This created havoc and people were duped for crores of rupees and did not have money for the marriages of their daughters or for medical treatment. Hazare agitated for over eight months. The result was that more than Rs 125 crore was recovered from defaulters and the members of such societies heaved a sigh of relief. Recovery of around Rs. 400 crores is in the pipeline.

In the future, the BVJA will work for the decentralisation of power and laws related to the same. Says Hazare, "we have decided to develop centers to create awareness amongst people about govt. schemes and train activists to know the

modus operandi of corruption in each sector. As the state government has decided to set up committees at almost every nodal point like state, district, tehsil, and village level with one member on such committee represented by our organisation. We have trained more than 400 volunteers to work on such committees."

Actually the government should train the members of NGOs who can work in the sector of prevention of corruption. Then and then only we can dream of corruption-free state, concludes Hazare.

Sustainable development of any village by making it a "Model Village" and eradication of corruption are two sides of the same coin. If both are adopted, only then there will be an established welfare state.

RIGHT TO INFORMATION MOVEMENT

In the early 2000s Hazare led a movement in Maharashtra state which forced the state government to pass a stronger Maharashtra Right to Information Act. This Act was later considered as the base document for the Right to Information Act 2005 (RTI), enacted by the Union Government. It also ensured that the President of India assented to this new Act. Law professor Alasdair Scott Roberts said:

> *The state of Maharashtra – home to one of the world's largest cities, Mumbai, adopted a Right to Information Act in 2003, prodded by the hunger strike of prominent activist, Anna Hazare. ("All corruption can end only if there is freedom of information," said Hazare, who resumed his strike in February 2004 to push for better enforcement of the Act).*

On 20 July 2006 the Union Cabinet amended the Right to Information Act 2005 to exclude the file noting by the government officials from its purview. Hazare began his fast unto death on 9 August 2006 in Alandi against the proposed amendment. He ended his fast on 19 August 2006, after the government agreed to change its earlier decision.

REGULATION OF TRANSFERS AND PREVENTION OF DELAY IN DISCHARGE OF OFFICIAL DUTIES ACT

Before 2006 in the state of Maharashtra, even honest government officers were transferred to other places according to ministers wish. Sometimes within months of being posted to a place, whereas some corrupt and favored officials were cozy in their postings for many years in some cases even for 10 to 20 years and since there was not any guideline or law many government officials were reluctant to process files that contained important public proposals and decisions. Anna fought hard for a law whereby a government servant must clear a file within a specified time and that transfers must take place only after three years. After many years of relentless efforts of Anna, finally on 25 May 2006 state government of Maharashtra issued a notification announcing that the execution of the special act, The Prevention of Delay in Discharge of Official Duties Act 2006, aimed at curbing the delay by its officers and employees in discharging their duties. This act provides for disciplinary action against officials who move files slowly and enables monitoring officials who stay too long in a post, or in a department, and for involvement in a corrupt nexus. Within this act, it is mandatory for the government to effect transfers of all government officers and employees, except Class IV workers, after the stipulated three years. Act also prevents the government from effecting frequent transfers of officers before the stipulated three-year tenure, except in case of emergency and under exceptional circumstances. Maharashtra is the first state in the country to have introduced such act. However, like others, this law has also not been followed in its true spirit.

CAMPAIGN AGAINST LIQUOR FROM FOOD GRAINS

Constitution of India Article 47 commits the State to raise the standard of living and improve public health, and prohibit the consumption of intoxicating drinks and drugs injurious to health.

In 2007 Maharashtra Government rolled out the grain-based liquor policy aimed to encourage production of liquor from food grain in the light of the rising demand for spirit—used for industrial purposes and potable liquor and

Issue 36 licenses for distilleries for making alcohol from food grains.

Anna Hazare opposed the governments policy to promote making liquor from food grains in Maharashtra. He argued the government that Maharashtra is a food-deficit State and there was shortage of food grains and it is not logical to promote producing liquor from food grains. One of the State ministers Laxman Dhoble said in his speech that those opposing the decision to allow use of food grains for the production of liquor are anti-farmers and those people should be beaten up with sugarcane sticks. Hazare initiated fast at Shirdi, but on March 21, 2010 government promised to review the policy and Anna ended his 5 day long fast. But the government later granted 36 licences and grants of ₹ 10 (US$0.22) (per litre of alcohol) to politicians or their sons who were directly or indirectly engaged in making alcohol from foodgrains. Some of the main beneficiaries of these licences includes Amit and Dheeraj Deshmukh, sons of Union Heavy Industries Minister Vilasrao Deshmukh, Bharatiya Janata Party leader Gopinath Munde's daughter Pankaja Palwe and her husband Charudatta Palwe, sons-in-law of P.V. Narasimha Rao, Rajya Sabha MP Govindrao Adik. The government approved the proposal for food grain-based alcohol production in spite of stiff opposition from the planning and finance departments saying there is a huge demand in other countries for food grain made liquor in comparison with that of molasses. Anna filed a Public Interest Litigation against the Government of Maharashtra for allowing food-grains for manufacturing liquor in the Nagpur bench of the Bombay High Court. On August 20, 2009 Maharashtra government stopped the policy. However, distilleries sanctioned before that date and those who started production within two years of sanction were entitled for subsidies.

On May 5, 2011 court refused to hear a Public Interest Litigation saying "not before me, this is a court of law, not a court of justice" as a reason of not hearing the plea. One of Principal Secretary in Maharashtra state C.S. Sangeet Rao, enlighten that there is no law exists to scrap these licences as this is a government policy.

4

Honours, Awards & Internatinal Recognition

Year of Award or Honor	Name of Award or Honor	Awarding Organization
2008	Jit Gill Memorial Award	World Bank
2005	Honorary Doctorate	Gandhigram Rural University, Dindigul, T.N.
2003	Integrity Award	Transparency International
2000	Giants International Awards	Shri Vilas Rao Deshmukh (CM, Maharastra)
1998	CARE International Award	CARE (relief agency)
1997	Mahaveer Puraskar	Bhagwan Mahaveer Foundation, Chennai
1996	Shiromani Award	P. A. Sangma (Speaker of Lok Sabha)
1992	Padma Bhushan	President of India
1990	Padma Shri	President of India
1989	Krishi Bhushana Award	Government of Maharashtra
1988	Man of the Year Award	
1986	Indira Priyadarshini Vrikshamitra Award	Government of India

5

Lokpal Bill Movement

"We are ready to get arrested and be beaten up but we have had enough of corruption. We are ready to sacrifice our lives"

–Anna Hazare

In March 2011, Hazare initiated a Satyagraha movement for passing a stronger anti-corruption Lokpal (Ombudsman) bill in the Indian Parliament as conceived in the Jan Lokpal Bill (People's Ombudsman Bill). The Jan Lokpal Bill was drafted earlier by N. Santosh Hegde, former justice of the Supreme Court of India and Lokayukta of Karnataka, Prashant Bhushan, a senior lawyer in the Supreme Court and Arvind Kejriwal, a social activist along with members of the India Against Corruption movement. This draft bill incorporated more stringent provisions and wider power to the Lokpal (Ombudsman) than the draft Lokpal Bill prepared by the government in 2010.

HUNGER STRIKE IN DELHI

Hazare began his fast unto death on 5 April 2011 at Jantar Mantar in Delhi to press for the demand to form a joint committee of the representatives of the Government and the civil society to draft a stronger anti-corruption bill with stronger penal actions and more independence to the Lokpal and Lokayuktas (Ombudsmen in the states), after his demand was rejected by the Prime Minister of India Manmohan Singh. He stated, "I will fast until Jan Lokpal Bill is passed".

Anna Hazare's hunger strike at Jantar Mantar in Delhi

The movement attracted attention in the media, and thousands of supporters. Almost 150 people reportedly joined Hazare in his fast. Social activists, including Medha Patkar, Arvind Kejriwal, former IPS officer Kiran Bedi, and Swami Agnivesh lent their support to Hazare's hunger strike and anti-corruption campaign. People have shown support in Internet social media such as Twitter and Facebook. Online Signature Campaigns like *avaaz* got 6.5lakh signatures in just 36 hours. In addition to spiritual leaders Sri Sri Ravi Shankar, Swami Ramdev, Swami Agnivesh and former Indian cricketer Kapil Dev, many celebrities showed their public support through Twitter. Hazare decided that he would not allow any politician to sit with him in this movement. Politicians like Uma Bharti and Om Prakash Chautala were shooed away by the protesters when they came to visit the site where the protest was taking place.

On 6 April 2011 Sharad Pawar resigned from the group of ministers formed for reviewing the draft Lokpal bill 2010.

The movement gathered significant support from India's youth, visible through the local support and on social networking sites like Facebook and Twitter. Protests spread to Bangalore, Mumbai, Chennai, Ahmedabad, Guwahati, Shillong, Aizawl and a number of other cities in India.

END OF HUNGER STRIKE AFTER MEETING DEMANDS

On 8 April 2011 the Government of India accepted all demands of the movement. On 9 April 2011 it issued a notification in the Gazette of India on formation of a joint committee. It accepted the formula that there be a politician Chairman and an activist, non-politician Co-Chairman. According to the notification, Pranab Mukherjee will be the Chairman of the draft committee while Shanti Bhushan will be the co-chairman. "The Joint Drafting Committee shall consist of five nominee ministers of the Government of India and five nominees of the civil society. The five nominee Ministers of the Government of India are Pranab Mukherjee, Union Minister of Finance, P. Chidambaram, Union Minister of Home Affairs, M. Veerappa Moily, Union Minister of Law and Justice, Kapil Sibal, Union Minister of Human Resource and Development and Minister of Communication and Information Technology and Salman Khursheed, Union Minister of Water Resources and Minister of Minority Affairs. The five nominees of the civil society are Anna Hazare, N. Santosh Hegde, Shanti Bhushan Senior Advocate, Prashant Bhushan, Advocate and Arvind Kejriwal.

On the morning of 9 April 2011 Hazare ended his 98-

hour hunger strike by first offering lemon juice to some of his supporters who were fasting with him. Hazare then broke his fast by consuming some lemon juice. He addressed the people and set a deadline of 15 August 2011 to pass the Lokpal Bill in the Indian Parliament.

"Real fight begins now. We have a lot of struggle ahead of us in drafting the new legislation, We have shown the world in just five days that we are united for the cause of the nation. The youth power in this movement is a sign of hope."

Anna Hazare said that if the bill does not pass he will call for a mass nation-wide agitation. He called his movement as "second struggle for independence" and he will continue the fight.

DIFFERENCES WITH THE GOVERNMENT ON DRAFT BILL

During the meeting of the joint drafting committee on 30 May 2011, the Union government members opposed the inclusion of the prime minister, higher judiciary and the acts of the MPs under the purview of the Lokpal in the draft bill. On 31 May 2011, Pranab Mukherjee, Chairman of the joint drafting committee sent a letter to the chief ministers of all states and the leaders of the political parties seeking their opinion on six contentious issues in the proposed Lokpal Bill, including whether to bring the prime minister and judges of Supreme Court and High Courts under the purview of the proposed law. But the civil society members of the drafting committee considered that keeping the prime minister and judges of Supreme Court and High Courts out of the purview of the Lokpal would be a violation of the United Nations Convention against Corruption.

Anna Hazare and other civil society members decided to boycott the meeting of the joint Lokpal Bill drafting committee scheduled on 6 June 2011 in protest against the forcible eviction of Swami Ramdev and his followers by the Delhi Police from Ramlila Maidan on 5 June 2011, while they were on hunger strike against the issues of black money and corruption and doubting seriousness of the government in taking measures to eradicate corruption.

On 6 June 2011, the members of the civil society of the joint Lokpal bill drafting committee in New Delhi sent a letter to Pranab Mukherjee, the chairman of the committee, explaining reasons for their absence at the meeting and also asked government to make its stand public on the contentious issues related to the proposed draft legislation. They also decided that the future meetings will be attended only if they were telecast live. On 8 June 2011 at Rajghat, describing his movement as the second freedom struggle, Anna criticized the Government for trying to discredit the joint Lokpal Bill drafting committee and threatened to go on indefinite fast again from 16 August 2011 if the Lokpal Bill is not passed by then. He also criticised the Government for putting hurdles in the drafting of a strong Lokpal Bill and its attempts to malign the civil society members of the joint Lokpal panel.

INDEFINITE FAST

On July 28, 2011 the union cabinet approved a draft of the Lokpal Bill, which keeps the Prime Minister, judiciary and lower bureaucracy out of the ambit of the proposed Lokpal.Hazare rejected the government version by describing it as "cruel joke" and wrote a letter to Prime Minister Manmohan Singh, and told him his decision to go on an indefinite fast from August 16, 2011 at Jantar

Mantar if the government introduced its own version of the bill in Parliament without taking suggestions from civil society members.

> *"Why are you (government) sending the wrong draft? We have faith in Parliament. But first send the right draft, our agitation is against government, not Parliament. The government has overlooked many points. How will it fight corruption by excluding government employees, CBI and prime minister from the Lokpal's purview? We were told that both the drafts would be sent to the Cabinet. But only the government's draft was sent. This is a deceitful government. They are lying. How will they run the country? Now I have no trust in this government. If it is really serious about fighting corruption, why is it not bringing government employees and CBI under Lokpal?"*
>
> –Anna Hazare

Within twenty four hours of cabinet's endorsement of a weak Lokpal Bill, over ten thousand peoples from across the country sent faxes directly to the government demanding a bill with stronger provisions.The Mumbai Taxi Men's Union, comprises over 30,000 taxi drivers have extended their full support to Hazare's fast by keeping all taxis off the roads on August 16, 2011. Lawyers of Allahabad High Court described Lokpal Bill proposed by the government as against the interest of the country and pledged their support to Hazare by hunger strike at Allahabad on August 16, 2011. On July 30, 2011 Vishwa Hindu Parishad supported Hazare's indefinite fast by saying movement for an effective anti-corruption ombudsman needs the backing of people.

ARREST AND AFTERMATH

On August 16 2011, Hazare was arrested four hours before the planned indefinite hunger strike. Rajan Bhagat, spokesman for Delhi Police said, police arrested Hazare under a legal provision that bans public gatherings and protests at the park in Delhi where he was planning to begin his hunger strike. Police took that action after Hazare refused to meet the conditions put forward by police for allowing the protest. The conditions included restricting the length of the fast to three days and the number of protesters at the site to 5,000. Later Anna was sent to Tihar Jail under judicial custody for 7 days.

Along with Hazare, other key members of the India Against Corruption movement including Arvind Kejriwal, Shanti Bhushan, Kiran Bedi and Manish Sisodia were also detained from different locations. It was reported that about 1,300 supporters were detained in Delhi. The arrest sparked off protests with people courting arrests in different parts of the country. The opposition parties in the country came out against the arrest, likening the government action to the emergency imposed in the country in 1975. Both the houses of Parliament were adjourned over the issue.

Eventually, after being kept in judicial detention for 24 hours, he was released by police, but Hazare and his supporters refused to sign bail bond and he was sent to Tihar Jail. They demanded permission to observe a fast in support of the Jan Lokpal bill, without any conditions. Hazare continued his fast inside the jail.

After his arrest, Anna Hazare received massive support from people across the country. Peaceful protest rallies and marches were held all over the country against the government's move of arresting Hazare and others. After protest by million of people across India the government finally agreed to release Anna Hazare from jail to begin public hunger strike which would last for fifteen days.

ELECTORAL REFORM MOVEMENT

In 2011, Anna Hazare demanded an amendment to the electoral law to incorporate the option of 'None of the above' in the electronic voting machines during the Indian elections. The "None of the above (NOTA)" is a ballot option that allows an electorate to indicate disapproval of all of the candidates in an electoral system, in case of non-availability of any candidate of his choice, as his Right to Reject. Soon, the Chief Election Commissioner of India Shahabuddin Yaqoob Quraishi supported Hazare's demand for the electoral reforms.

PROTEST AGAINST ATROCITIES AGAINST SWAMI RAMDEV AND HIS SUPPORTERS

> *"How can the government stop anyone from protesting? The land is not their 'father's property'. The citizens are the masters of this country and the ministers are their servants"."*
>
> –Anna Hazare

On 8 June 2011, Anna Hazare and thousands of his supporters observed fast from 10 am to 6 pm at Rajghat to protest against the midnight crackdown of 5 June 2011 by the Delhi Police on Swami Ramdev's fast at Ramlila Maidan, New Delhi. The fast was initially planned to be held at Jantar Mantar, but the venue was shifted after the denial of permission by the Delhi police. Anna Hazare held the Prime Minister of India responsible for the atrocities and termed the police action as a blot on humanity and an attempt to stifle democracy. According to one of the Anna's young supporters, the large presence of youths in the protest was due to their support to his use of nonviolence means of protest similar to Gandhi.

6
Indian Anti-Corruption Movement, 2011

The 2011 Indian freedom struggle against corruption refers to a series of protests against the Government of India intended to seek strong legislation against graft, otherwise known as corruption. The protests have centred on a proposed bill, called the Jan Lokpal Bill, which the protestors believe could address the issue if it was suitably worded and enforced. The movement has gained momentum in particular since 5 April 2011, when Anna Hazare, first went on a hunger strike which he called a "fast unto death".

The protesters are of the opinion that the government desires to dilute proposals contained in the original draft of the Jan Lokpal bill. They believe that the changes would make the body intended to oversee the issue, the Lokayukta, no more than a powerless advisory body in the Indian bureaucracy. Hazare, who is a Gandhian, went on his initial hunger strike when talks designed to consider the issues broke down. He had demanded the creation of a joint drafting committee for the bill, with members from both "civil society" and government.

Following Hazare's initial, much publicised protest action, a second major protest saw controversial events take place at the Ramlila Maidan, New Delhi on 4 June 2011. The figurehead for these protests was Swami Ramdev and their aim was to highlight the need for strong legislation to bring back to the country what has been called "black money" deposited abroad. Ramdev demanded that untaxed money invested abroad should be declared to be the wealth of the nation. Further, that the act of caching money, which is alleged to have been obtained illegally, in foreign banks should be declared a crime against the state. He also demanded that the nation's wealth held in foreign banks should be brought back and that India should sign the United Nations Convention against Corruption. It is estimated that around US$ 350 billion to US$ 1400 billion worth of illegal money is in foreign banks.

The protests led to the creation of a movement that saw protests being organised in various cities and towns of India. Protests included fasts, candlelight vigils and rallies. The protests are unusual in India as they have no political affiliation and the protesters have been hostile to any attempt by political parties to use them to strengthen their own political agenda.

BACKGROUND

Issues regarding corruption in India have become more prominent in recent years. The country was subject to socialist-inspired economic policies between the 1950s and the late 1980s. Extensive regulation, protectionism, and public ownership led to slow growth. Forbes commented in 2007 that the system of bureaucratic controls called License Raj was often at the core of corruption.

The Vohra Report of 1993, submitted by the former Indian Union Home Secretary N. N. Vohra, studied the problem of the criminalization of politics and of the nexus among criminals, politicians and bureaucrats in India. The report contained several observations made by official agencies on the criminal network which was virtually running a parallel government. It also discussed criminal gangs who enjoyed the patronage of politicians—of all political parties—and the protection of government functionaries. It revealed that political leaders had become the leaders of gangs. They were also connected to the military. Over the years criminals had been elected to local bodies, State Assemblies, and even the Parliament.

The Right to Information Act of 2005 has helped civilians work effectively towards tackling corruption. It allows Indian citizens (except those living in Jammu and Kashmir) to request information, for a fixed fee of ₹ 10 (US$ 0.22), from a "public authority" (a body of Government or "instrumentality of State") which is required to reply expeditiously or within thirty days. Activists have used this to uncover graft cases against various politicians and bureaucrats, one consequence being that some of those activists have been attacked and even killed.

Various scandals were discovered in the period 2010-2011, including the 2G spectrum scam, Adarsh Housing Society scam, and the Commonwealth Games scam. These involved various Ministers and also members of the Armed Forces, and they demonstrated how entrenched corruption had become in India. They led also to popular, non-political movements campaigning to fight graft via new legislation.

The Jan Lokpal Bill is a proposal to establish an independent body to investigate cases of corruption within a year and to ensure a speedy prosecution within two years of an investigation being started. The Jan Lokpal Bill was proposed by members of the civil society (primarily social activists from the NGO India Against Corruption) as an alternative to the Government-drafted Lokpal Bill. The August 16 protests started as a result of significant disagreements over the two versions of the Bill between the civil society leaders and the Government.

PROTEST TIMELINE

A group of Delhi residents drove around the city dressed in similar clothing in an attempt to raise awareness of corruption issues and to gain support for the Jan Lokpal Bill.

28 March 2011

There were protest marches in various cities across the world, including some in the US. These included a 240-mile march in California that had begun on 12 March in San Diego and ended on 26 March at the statue erected in honour of Gandhi in San Francisco.

30 March 2011

Kapil Dev, a former captain of the Indian national cricket team, wrote a letter to the Prime Minister, Manmohan Singh, complaining that the many investigations into scams arising from the recent Commonwealth Games had achieved nothing so far. He said that, "Why can't we have an independent Lokpal to look into these scams. I consider you as the cleanest politician in the recent history and I urge you for a Jan Lokpal Bill."

4 April 2011

Hazare announced that he would commence his "fast unto death" and that this would last until a comprehensive measure to tackle corruption was introduced. He claimed that the government had excluded "civil society" from the panel set up to draft the Jan Lokpal Bill and implied that at least one of the people who was to be on the drafting committee–Sharad Pawar–might be unsuitable for that role because of his large landholdings. Kiran Bedi and Swami Agnivesh voiced their support for Hazare.

5 April 2011

Hazare initiated his fast at Jantar Mantar in Delhi. Elsewhere, people attended a protest at Freedom Park, Bangalore.

Campaigners for India Against Corruption (IAC) estimated that a petition circulated in the city of Pune which demanded that the government enact a bill had attracted between 5000 and 6000 signatures between 3 April and 5 April. Hazare has been involved with IAC, a group established by various prominent activists with the primary purpose of achieving the legal enactment and subsequent enforcement of a strong version of the Jan Lokpal bill.

7 April 2011

Two rounds of talks failed. There was agreement regarding constituting a panel to examine the Bill but the government would not accede to demands that it should be a formally constituted panel or that Hazare should lead it. As a consequence of this, Hazare continued his fast.

Narendra Modi, the Chief Minister of Gujarat lashes out at Manmohan Singh for resisting the passage of the Jan Lokpal Bill.

Sonia Gandhi, the president of the Indian National Congress party and the head of the National Advisory Council appealed to Hazare to end his indefinite fast.

Hazare and the protesters tried to keep the protests non-political. No politicians were welcome at the site of the fast.

Former Haryana Chief Minister Om Prakash Chautala, former Madhya Pradesh Chief Minister Uma Bharti and pro Sonia Gandhi journalist Barkha Dutt were forced by civilians to leave, after the protesters objected against their presence which they believed was harming the integrity of their movement.

8 April 2011

Protests spread to numerous other places, including Mumbai, Kolkata, Thiruvananthapuram, Hyderabad, Jaipur, Chennai, Patna, Bhopal, Ahmedabad, Ranchi, Pune, and the University of Jammu.

The government continued to squabble with the activists stating that the bill drafting committee will be headed by a government appointed minister and not a civil society member as the protesters demanded to avoid allowing the government to make the bill less powerful.

The Prime Minister, Manmohan Singh, met with the President of India to outline to her how the government was going ahead with the demands of the population.

15 supporters of Hazare on fast were hospitalized.

Bollywood came out in support of the protests, with actors, musicians and directors speaking in support of the movement and Hazare. Director Farah Khan, actor Anupam Kher, music director Vishal Dadlani, poet-filmmaker Pritish Nandy and actor Tom Alter all visited Jantar Mantar; others stated their support for the movement via social networking websites or the media. Oscar winning Indian composer A. R. Rahman also declared his support for the anti-graft movement.

Indian students at Cambridge University, the former *alma mater* of the Indian prime minister also expressed their support for the movement.

Many prominent people from the government agencies as well as from various corporate houses came out in support of the movement. Some of them were–Delhi Metro chief E. Sreedharan (also called the Metro Man of India), Punj Lloyd Chairman Atul Punj, Maruti Suzuki Chairman R. C. Bhargava, Hero group's Sunil Munjal, Tata Steel Vice-chairman B Muthuraman, Bajaj Auto Chairman Rahul Bajaj, Godrej Group Head Adi Godrej, Biocon Chairman and Managing Director Kiran Mazumdar-Shaw and Kotak Mahindra Bank Vice-chairman & Managing Director Uday Kotak. They all declared their support for Hazare and the movement.

ASSOCHAM President Dilip Modi and FICCI Director General Rajiv Kumar, too came out in support of the movement.

The Government of India accepted the compromise formula that there be a politician Chairman and an activist, non-politician Co-chairman. It was reported that Pranab Mukherjee will be the Chairman of the draft committee while Shanti Bhushan will be the Co-chairman. Bhushan was one of the original drafters of the Lokpal Bill along with Hazare, Justice N. Santosh Hegde, advocate Prashant Bhushan, and RTI activist Arvind Kejriwal.

9 April 2011

After accepting all the demands of Hazare, the Government of India issued a Official Gazette saying that the draft of lokpal would be made and presented in the coming monsoon session of Lok Sabha.

Victory celebrations took place throughout the country. and even Hazare's village.

Protesters and leaders of the movement alike stated that the path to attaining complete passing of the bill is still a difficult one, and the movement has to see more harsher days ahead.

Many commentators have called the movement the 'wake-up' call for India.

Within a day of the beginning of the agitation, more than 30,000 people had pledged their support to the Lokpal Bill. Organisers of the India Against Corruption said 30,000 people from Maharashtra expressed their support on their website. The website has 20,000 members in Mumbai alone. Within a few days the Facebook page for India Against Corruption had more than 220,000 likes.

16 April 2011

The first meeting regarding a draft of the Lokpal Bill was held on 16 April. The government agreed to audio-record all meetings of the Lokpal Bill panel and to hold public consultations before a final draft is prepared. Hazare demanded that the proceedings be televised live but the government refused.

4 June 2011

Swami Ramdev begins his indefinite hunger strike at Ramlila Maidan in New Delhi to bring back the black money stashed in tax havens abroad.

65,000 followers gathered at Ramlila Maidan.

In a press conference in the evening Kapil Sibbal made public a letter from Ramdev's camp to call off the hunger strike. Ramdev took it as a betrayal and hardened position.

5 June 2011

At midnight, police raided the ground when most protesters were sleeping and Swami Ramdev was busy at a meeting with his core group.

A large police force lobbed tear gas shells, and lathicharged the crowd at 1 am (IST) to evict them.

Police had arranged buses to drop supporters at railway stations and bus stands in advance; had ammunition ready and were in battle-gear wearing vests and helmets and kept some ambulances on standby.

Delhi Police arrested Ramdev, who was disguised in a salwar kameez with a group of female protesters heading peacefully towards the New Delhi Railway Station

Ramdev is held in a government guesthouse for a few hours and then sent to Dehradun in a BSF aircraft.

Ramdev is sent to his Patanjali Yogpeeth ashram in Haridwar where he delivers a press conference.

Ramdev is prohibited from entering Delhi for 15 days.

9 June 2011

Hazare describes his fight against corruption as the "Second Freedom Struggle" and set an ultimatum of 15 August 2011, as the last date to pass a strong Jan Lokpal Bill threatening to otherwise intensify his anti-corruption agitation and start another fast from 16 August.

16 June 2011

The Government and the civil society split wide open due to differences in jointly drafting bill. Government representatives informed that if a consensus on the common bill is not reached, two drafts will be sent to the Cabinet, one drafted by the Government and the other drafted by the civil society. Team Anna also claimed that only 15 points out of total 71 recommended were agreed and included in the joint draft. Hazare declared that if the government version of the bill was passed in the Parliament, he will start his hunger strike from August 16, 2011.

15 August 2011

Anna Hazare announced at a press conference that he and his supporters are determined to go ahead with his fast on 16 August, 2011 as planned. He also urged people to court arrest to push for a stronger Lokpal bill.

Section 144 was imposed a night before the planned protest date, at JP Park, Rajghat and Dilli Gate, which prohibits assembly of five or more persons.

16 August 2011

Anna Hazare was detained by Delhi Police early morning before he could start his hunger strike at JP Park, Delhi. Delhi Police had asked Anna not to leave his home, the request which was declined by the later, and hence was detained at outside the residence of lawyer Prashant Bhushan in Mayur Vihar. Arvind Kejriwal, Kiran Bedi, Manish Sisodia and more than 1200 supporters were also taken to preventive custody by the Police.

Anna Hazare was sent to seven days judicial custody to Tihar Jail for refusing to sign a personal bond and come out on bail.

Shehla Masood, an RTI activist and a strong supporter of Anna Hazare's anti-corruption movement, was shot dead in front of her house in Koh-e-Fiza, Bhopal.

Kiran Bedi and Shanti Bhushan, detained by Delhi Police on morning ahead of Anna Hazare's fast-unto-death, were released in the evening at around 6:30pm IST.

Current telecom minister Kapil Sibal was greeted with black flags and booed by a group of students at a seminar on the Jan Lokpal bill.

With Government of India, preparing to release Anna Hazare late night within a day itself, however the later refused to come out of Tihar jail until the government agrees for an unconditional permission to hold protests at JP Park.

The atmosphere outside Tihar Jail has been charged all day, all eyes fixed for hours on the gate that Anna Hazare will reportedly emerge from. Supporters have raised slogans in support of Mr Hazare and sung songs and bhajans. They also fell silent for a while in wait for the moment when Anna Hazare would walk out.

Many supporters camped outside the jail overnight to show solidarity with Anna's cause; many more have been gathering there since early morning, as they have been at Chhatrasal Stadium in north Delhi, which was deemed "jail" by Delhi Police on August 16, 2011 to hold the over 1000 anti-corruption protesters detained in the Capital. Yoga teacher and anti-corruption activist Baba Ramdev too visited Tihar and then the Chattrasal Stadium after he met the President to submit a memorandum against Anna's arrest this morning.

17 August 2011

After almost a day, Anna still refuses to leave jail and spent night in a room in Tihar jail, despite the government decision to free him.

August 19

Hazare leaves Tihar Jail, goes to Ramlila Maidan, on the way paying homage to Mahatma Gandhi at Rajghat and Amar Jawan Jyoti in a big proccession, continues to fast at Ramlila Maidan, New Delhi.

The Ramlila Maidan, is a large ground located in the middle of the city of Delhi. Located inside the walled city, the Ramlila Maidan is walled on all sides, has two large gates and is very well maintained, it even has a pond in the middle. The Ramlila Grounds are popular because every year during Dusshera, the demon king Ravana's effigy is burned here and Ramlila is performed here everyday during this period.

The Ramlila Maidan is located near the New Delhi Railway Station and Delhi Gate. These grounds have been in the news a lot lately because of Baba Ramdev's campaign against black money there in June, 2011 and Anna Hazare's hunger strike against corruption in August 2011.

August 21

Anna Hazare asked his supporters to sit on *Dharna* outside the residences of members of parliament and union ministers all over India.

August 23

Government invites Team Anna for talks.

August 24

Second round of talks, all-party meeting held. No breakthrough in impasse.

August 25

After meetings with political parties and Team Anna, government agrees to debate all versions of Lokpal bill in parliament.

August 26

Hazare tells Prime Minister that he may end his fast if three of his key demands are met.

August 27

Parliament debate Lokpal bill, adjourn after adopting 'sense of the house' and agreeing to Hazare's three demands that will be sent to standing committee on Lokpal bill.

Both houses of Parliament passed a resolution conveying the sense of the House on the Lokpal Bill, paving the way for Anna Hazare to break his fast. On a motion moved by Pranab Mukherjee, Lok Sabha and Rajya Sabha passed a resolution conveying the sense of the House on the Lokpal Bill.

August 28

Anna breaks fast on 13th day by drinking coconut water with honey wihch was offered by two little girls Simran and Ikra.

Anna Hazare announced his roadmap for the near future, saying: 'I have only suspended my agitation. I will not rest until all the changes that I look to are achieved.' he also made it clear that his struggle to rid the Indian system of corruption would continue.

He immediately announced his next target: sweeping reforms to the election and education systems, and a campaign to improve the livelihoods of millions of farmers and labourers. He also gave a sneak preview of his ideas on electoral reform, saying his next campaign would be based

around the idea of the 'right to recall and right to reject.'

The right to recall would cover elected representatives of the people, while the right to reject would mean a column on the ballot paper allowing the voter to say that he or she doesn't like the listed candidates. 'If the majority say they don't like any of the candidates in the fray, the election should be cancelled.'

Both houses of parliament unanimously adopted a resolution without actually having to vote on his three demands.

'The House discussed various issues relating to the setting up of a strong and effective Lokpal. This House agrees in principle on the following issues for an effective and strong Lokpal: 1) Citizen's charter, 2) Lower bureaucracy under Lokpal through appropriate mechanism, 3) Establishment of Lokayukta in states, 4) Further resolve to forward the proceedings of the House to the Standing Committee for its perusal while formulating its recommendations for a Lokpal Bill.'

Thousands of Hazare's national flag-waving supporters at the Ramlila ground shouted slogans in support as two young girls, Simran and Ikrah, offered him honey mixed with coconut water at 10.20 am on Sunday. Hazare was flanked by his team as he made his victory speech, in which he said that what civil society achieved in parliament on Saturday was indeed a victory for the people of India. 'This movement has created a faith that the country can be rid of corruption and we can go ahead with implementing laws and the Constitution,' he said.

Hazare exhorted the crowds to continue their non-violent fight against corruption, saying the battle had just begun. 'You don't become Anna by wearing the Anna cap. You become Anna by practicing my principles,' he told his supporters.

After his brief speech, a visibly elated but frail Hazare was driven straight to Gurgaon by his personal doctor Naresh Trehan and admitted to the Medanta Medicity hospital, where he was kept under round-the-clock observation for three days.

BACKGROUND

On July 18, 2011, Hazare declared that he had written a letter to Prime Minister informing him about his decision to go on an indefinite fast from August 16 at Jantar Mantar. Hazare said that it was the right of Indian citizens to protest and the government could not crush their movement unlike the Ramlila ground protests. Hazare declared that he was ready to get arrested and beaten up and informed the Delhi Police about his protest.

Hazare's crusade for a strong Lokpal Bill found support in Mumbai as the Mumbai Taximen's Union, comprising over 30,000 taxis, agreed to extend their support to

Hazare's cause on August 16. The union's decision came after a meeting with Hazare's team in Mumbai. The union's proposal was to keep all taxis off the roads or ply less number of taxis on August 16. The Mumbai chapter of India Against Corruption claimed that till July 26, nearly 44,000 people had shown interest in joining the protest from August 16.

In Allahabad, the legal community expressed their support in Hazare's campaign against corruption. Lawyers of Allahabad High Court held protests in support of Anna Hazare at Allahabad by burning copies of Lokpal Bill, blocking roads and raising slogans against the callus carefree of the government and also pledged to go on hunger strike at Allahabad from August 16 in support of Anna Hazare.

The Vishwa Hindu Parishad also came out in support of Hazare's movement, saying that for a strong Lokpal, people from across the country should support the campaign.

In a referendum conducted by India Against Corruption in Karnataka, about 94.3% of Chikkaballapur constituency and 79.7% of Bangalore South voted to bring the prime minister under the ambit of the Jan Lokpal Bill. The results showed that a majority of the population wanted the Jan Lokpal Bill to be passed by the Parliament and not the "watered down, toothless" Bill drafted by the government. The 6,000 participants at the referendum also said that being representatives of the people, members of parliament should vote for the Lokpal, not as per party directives but as per the voice of the majority in his/her constituency. The participants also voted to bring judges under Lokpal, give adequate powers to the Lokpal to dismiss officers guilty of corruption, monitor corruption at the central as well as state level through Lokayuktas and to bring all levels of officers under the Bill. The questionnaire had a set of eight questions that brought out crucial differences between the Jan Lokpal Bill and the Lokpal Bill put forth by the government and asked for the people's vote on the same. Around ten parliamentary constituencies across the nation conducted a similar exercise and the results from the nation-wide campaign will be consolidated and presented to the members of the Parliament in time for the monsoon session.

HAZARE'S ARREST

On the morning of August 16, 2011, Hazare, along with close associates, was remanded to judicial custody for seven days. Hazare revived his hunger protest for a strong Lokpal, even after the Delhi police detained him in the wee hours of August 16. Hazare was picked up by police at about 7.30am from a residence in east Delhi for "intending to defy prohibitory orders". Late afternoon, he was produced before a special executive magistrate. After he refused to sign a personal bond to be allowed to get out on bail he was remanded in judicial custody for seven days. Within hours of his detention, a spokesperson for Team Anna said that he had begun his hunger protest while in police custody and that he was not accepting even water to drink. The arrest of Hazare and some of his close associates, set off a groundswell of protests across the country and this appeared to be spreading quickly. The arrest was condemned by political parties, the chief ministers of some non-Congress ruled states, non-government organizations and even parliament did not transact any business after an uproar on the issue forced an adjournment for the day.

As protests built up in several cities and towns over the arrest, Prashant Bhushan, one of Hazare's key associates, announced a march from India Gate to Parliament House on Wednesday to protest against the police action, which he described was taken at the behest of some cabinet ministers. Delhi police commissioner BK Gupta said that the police was not keen that Hazare be sent to judicial custody. He said police was prepared to release him on a personal bond if he would have given an undertaking that he would not defy Section 144 of the Criminal Procedure Code which prohibits the gathering of five or more people and ask his supporters not to do so also. Hazare was taken to the Tihar jail where he will spend the time in judicial custody. Kiran Bedi, Arvind Kejriwal and Manoj Sisodia, three other leading activists of Team Anna, have also been sent to judicial custody on similar grounds. In a message released after his detention, Hazare said this was the beginning of the "second freedom struggle" and he called on people to participate in a "jail bharo" agitation.

Opposition parties, peeved over the attitude of the Congress in parliament, said they would meet later today to decide on the course of action. Communist Party of India leader Gurudas Dasgupta said he had proposed a boycott of parliament for three days. Communist Party of India (Marxist) leader Brinda Karat described the arrest as "a strong attack on democratic rights". Hours after arrest of Hazare, Leader of Opposition in Lok Sabha and BJP leader Sushma Swaraj strongly condemned the action and demanded and explanation from Prime Minister, Manmohan Singh saying that the government is hell-bent on crushing the civil rights of the citizens. Senior Bhartiya Janata Party leader L K Advani said he was not surprised at the detention of Mr Hazare and he charged the government with looking for scapegoats and stopping peaceful protests instead of fighting corruption. Arun Jaitley, leader of the opposition in the Rajya Sabha, said, that it was a very sad day for Indian democracy, where the ruling government took away the right to protest and the right to dissent.

In Patna, Bihar chief minister Nitish Kumar described the detention of Hazare and his associates as a "rehearsal of emergency" which people will never tolerate, and "a murder of democracy." Punjab chief minister Prakash Singh Badal also condemned the arrests saying that the Congress has panicked over the movement of Anna Hazare and accused Congress leaders of stashing money abroad. In Chandigarh and Ludhiana, people from all walks of life took to the streets - despite inclement weather - to join the protest for a strong Lokpal. Among them were activists of the NGOs 'India Against Corruption' and 'Awaaz' who launched a relay hunger strike. Traffic was also blocked at several intersections. Slamming the Centre for detaining Anna Hazare and his aides, Bihar Deputy Chief Minister SK Modi today called upon the people to come to the streets to hold demonstration in support of Anna's movement against corruption "peacefully and democratically."

In Hyderabad, Telugu Desam Party president N. Chandrababu Naidu asked the Prime minister Manmohan Singh to apologize to the nation for having sent Hazare and other social activists, who are fighting against corruption, to Tihar jail. In Maharashtra, crowds gathered in many cities and towns in response to Mr Hazare's call to court arrest. Thousands poured into south Mumbai's Azad Maidan since early in the morning, in preparation for the *'Jail Bharo'* programme. A large number of people courted arrest in support of the demand for an effective Lokpal. Many people wearing 'Gandhi' caps with slogans 'I am Anna' gathered at the Reserve Bank of India Square, on the busy Nagpur-Jabalpur national highway that runs through the Civil Lines area.

In a broad day light murder at Bhopal, capital of Madhya Pradesh, an RTI activist and a strong supporter of Anna Hazare's anti-corruption movement, Shehla Masood was shot dead around 11.30 am on August 16. An unidentified assailant shot her dead from point blank range while she was leaving in her car to attend a demonstration in support of Anna Hazare.

In Delhi, in protest against the arrest of Anna Hazare and his close aides by the Delhi Police, the members of All India Students Association showed black flags and shouted anti-government slogan against Kapil Sibal, who was to address a seminar at Malvankar Hall in city.

Anna on August 16 asked government employees across the country to go on mass leave to show solidarity with the movement. Union Home minister P. Chidambaram hoped they would not respond, describing the call as "completely wrong." Hazare's close associate and lawyer Prashant Bhushan urged government servants to join their cause and take a mass leave for a day and join the protests in their city.

RELEASE

After protests all over India, the UPA government forced a decision to release Hazare barely hours after he had been sent to Tihar Jail for seven days. Hazare had even refused food and water intake in Tihar jail, indicating he would carry on his fast in jail. Hazare and his aides including, Kiran Bedi and Arvind Kejriwal, were first taken to the Delhi Police Officer's Mess in North Delhi and were shifted to another after Hazare's supporters gathered in large numbers at Civil Lines. The Delhi Police sent a warrant to the Tihar Jail for the release of Hazare and his supporters withdrawing bail bond conditions, which Hazare had earlier refused to sign. Over 1,500 people who have been detained for taking part in protests demanding Hazare's release are also likely to be released at 9:30pm (IST). Congress sources said that the Government decided to release Hazare and his supporters after coming to the conclusion that keeping him in jail would create unnecessary law and order problem. The decision to release Hazare was taken after Prime Minister Manmohan Singh met party General Secretary Rahul Gandhi on Tuesday evening where Rahul disapproved of the arrest. Hazare supporters Kiran Bedi and Shanti Bhushan were released by the Delhi Police early on August 16. Hazare and Sisodia had been kept in Jail No. 4 of Tihar Jail where Congress MP and Commonwealth Games scam accused Suresh Kalmadi is also lodged. Kejriwal and others have been sent to Jail No. 1 where DMK leader and former telecom minister A Raja, who is accused of being involved in the 2G spectrum scam, lodged. However on release, Anna Hazare refused to come out of Tihar jail until the government agrees for an unconditional permission to hold protests at JP Park.

On August 18, 2011 Delhi Police gave permission to sit on hunger strike for 15 days only at Ramlila Maidan. Anna Hazare left Tihar Jail on August 19, 2011 at 11.45 IST and went to Rajghat to pay homage to Mahatma Gandhi before launching his protest against corruption at Ramlila Maidan.

(see page. 55-58)

7

Right to Information Act, 2005

The Right to Information Act 2005 (RTI) is an Act of the Parliament of India "to provide for setting out the practical regime of right to information for citizens." The Act applies to all States and Union Territories of India, except the State of Jammu and Kashmir–which is covered under a State-level law. Under the provisions of the Act, any citizen (excluding the citizens within J&K) may request information from a "public authority" (a body of Government or "instrumentality of State") which is required to reply expeditiously or within thirty days. The Act also requires every public authority to computerize their records for wide dissemination and to pro-actively publish certain categories of information so that the citizens need minimum recourse to request for information formally. This law was passed by Parliament on 15 June 2005 and came fully into force on 13 October 2005. Information disclosure in India was hitherto restricted by the Official Secrets Act 1923 and various other special laws, which the new RTI Act now relaxes.

FRAMEWORK

Disclosure of State information in British India was (and is) governed from 1889 by the Official Secrets Act. This law secures information related to security of the

State, sovereignty of the country and friendly relations with foreign states, and contains provisions which prohibit disclosure of non-classified information. Civil Service conduct rules and the Indian Evidence Act impose further restrictions on government officials' powers to disclose information to the public.

FREEDOM OF INFORMATION ACT 2002

Passage of a national level law, however, proved to be a difficult task. Given the experience of state governments in passing practicable legislation, the Central Government appointed a working group under H. D. Shourie and assigned it the task of drafting legislation. The Shourie draft, in an extremely diluted form, was the basis for the Freedom of Information Bill, 2000 which eventually became law under the Freedom of Information Act, 2002. This Act was severely criticized for permitting too many exemptions, not only under the standard grounds of national security and sovereignty, but also for requests that would involve "disproportionate diversion of the resources of a public authority". There was no upper limit on the charges that could be levied. There were no penalties for not complying with a request for information. The FoI Act, consequently, never came into effective force.

STATE LEVEL LAWS

The RTI Laws were first successfully enacted by the state governments of – Tamil Nadu (1997), Goa (1997), Rajasthan (2000), Karnataka (2000), Delhi (2001), Maharashtra (2002), Assam (2002), Madhya Pradesh (2003), and Jammu and Kashmir (2004). The Maharashtra and Delhi State level enactments are considered to have been the most widely used. The Delhi RTI Act is still in force. Jammu & Kashmir, has its own Right to Information Act of 2009, the successor to the repealed J&K Right to Information Act, 2004 and its 2008 amendments.

RIGHT TO INFORMATION MOVEMENT

In the mid-1990s, under Aruna Roy's guidance, the Mazdoor Kisan Shakti Sangathana MKSS began a campaign that advocated the public's right to scrutinize official records, a crucial check against arbitrary governance. The MKSS attacked corruption at the grassroots level and sought accountability of public officials in matters related to disbursement of government funds. The fact that the MKSS was founded and led by a woman activist, namely Aruna, commended the organization and its cause to the favour of Sonia Gandhi. Aruna leveraged this advantage further by ingenuously linking the Right to Information with issues related to women's employment, livelihood and empowerment. With Sonia Gandhi's support, the Congress-led government of Rajasthan passed the Rajasthan Right to Information Bill in 2000. Rajasthan, never otherwise noted for its progressive outlook, passed such a legislation, and Aruna received the Ramon Magsaysay Award for Community Leadership the same year. Aruna decided to use the award money of US $ 50,000 to set up a trust to support the process of democratic struggles.

In 2004, under the leadership of Sonia Gandhi, the Congress party won the national elections and formed the central government. Aruna was inducted into the National Advisory Committee (NAC), an extremely powerful but extra-constitutional quasi-governmental body headed by Sonia Gandhi which effectively supervises the working of the common minimum program of UPA II . Aruna's role was to formulate the Right to Information Act which was passed by the Indian parliament in 2005. She served as a member of the National Advisory Council of India until 2006 and is part of NAC II.

In the early 2000s Anna Hazare led a movement in Maharashtra state which forced the state government to pass a stronger Maharashtra Right to Information Act. This Act was later considered as the base document for the Right to Information Act 2005 (RTI), enacted by the Union Government. It also ensured that the President of India assented to this new Act. Law professor Alasdair Scott Roberts said:

The state of Maharashtra–home to one of the world's largest cities, Mumbai, adopted a Right to Information Act in 2003, prodded by the hunger strike of prominent activist, Anna Hazare. ("All corruption can end only if there is freedom of information," said Hazare, who resumed his strike in February 2004 to push for better enforcement of the Act).

On 20 July 2006 the Union Cabinet amended the Right to Information Act 2005 to exclude the file noting by the government officials from its purview. Hazare began his fast unto death on 9 August 2006 in Alandi against the proposed amendment. He ended his fast on 19 August 2006, after the government agreed to change its earlier decision.

SCOPE

The Act covers the whole of India except Jammu and Kashmir, where J&K Right to Information Act is in force. It is applicable to all constitutional authorities, including the executive, legislature and judiciary; any institution or body established or constituted by an act of Parliament or a state legislature. It is also defined in the Act that bodies or authorities established or constituted by order or notification of appropriate government including bodies "owned, controlled or substantially financed" by government, or non-Government organizations "substantially financed, directly or indirectly by funds" provided by the government are also covered in it.

PRIVATE BODIES

Private bodies are not within the Act's ambit directly. However, information that can be accessed under any other law in force by a public authority can also be requested. In a landmark decision of 30-Nov-2006 ('Sarbajit Roy versus DERC') the Central Information Commission also reaffirmed that privatised public utility companies continue to be within the RTI Act- their privatisation notwithstanding.

The Act specifies that citizens have a right to:

* request any information (as defined).
* obtain copies of documents.
* inspect documents, works and records.
* take certified samples of materials of work.

PROCESS

Under the Act, all authorities covered must appoint their Public Information Officer (PIO). Any person may submit a request to the PIO for information in writing. It is the PIO's obligation to provide information to citizens of India who request information under the Act. If the request pertains to another public authority (in whole or part) it is the PIO's responsibility to transfer/forward the concerned portions of the request to a PIO of the other within 5 days. In addition, every public authority is required to designate Assistant Public Information Officers (APIOs) to receive

RTI requests and appeals for forwarding to the PIOs of their public authority. The applicant is not required to disclose any information or reasons other than his name and contact particulars to seek the information.

The Act specifies time limits for replying to the request.

* If the request has been made to the PIO, the reply is to be given within 30 days of receipt.
* If the request has been made to an APIO, the reply is to be given within 35 days of receipt.
* If the PIO transfers the request to another public authority (better concerned with the information requested), the time allowed to reply is 30 days but computed from the day after it is received by the PIO of the transferee authority.
* Information concerning corruption and Human Rights violations by scheduled Security agencies (those listed in the Second Schedule to the Act) is to be provided within 45 days but with the prior approval of the Central Information Commission.
* However, if life or liberty of any person is involved, the PIO is expected to reply within 48 hours.

Since the information is to be paid for, the reply of the PIO is necessarily limited to either denying the request (in whole or part) and/or providing a computation of "further fees". The time between the reply of the PIO and the time taken to deposit the further fees for information is excluded from the time allowed.

If information is not provided within this period, it is treated as deemed refusal. Refusal with or without reasons may be ground for appeal or complaint. Further, information not provided in the times prescribed is to be provided free of charge.

For Central Departments as of 2006, there is a fee of ₹ 10 for filing the request, ₹ 2 per page of information and ₹ 5 for each hour of inspection after the first hour. If the applicant is a Below Poverty Card holder, then no fee shall apply. Such BPL Card holders have to provide a copy of their BPL card along with their application to the Public Authority. States Government and High Courts fix their own rules.

PARTIAL DISCLOSURE

The Act allows those part(s) of the record which are not exempt from disclosure and which can reasonably be severed from parts containing exempt information to be provided.

Exclusions

Central Intelligence and Security agencies specified in the Second Schedule like IB, RAW, Central Bureau of Investigation (CBI), Directorate of Revenue Intelligence, Central Economic Intelligence Bureau, Directorate of Enforcement, Narcotics Control Bureau, Aviation Research Centre, Special Frontier Force, BSF, CRPF, ITBP, CISF, NSG, Assam Rifles, Special Service Bureau, Special Branch (CID), Andaman and Nicobar, The Crime Branch-CID-CB, Dadra and Nagar Haveli and Special Branch, Lakshadweep Police. Agencies specified by the State Governments through a Notification will also be excluded. The exclusion, however, is not absolute and these organizations have an obligation to provide information pertaining to allegations of corruption and human rights violations. Further, information relating to allegations of human rights violation could be given but only with the approval of the Central or State Information Commission

INFORMATION EXCLUSIONS

The following is exempt from disclosure [S.8)]

* Information, disclosure of which would prejudicially affect the sovereignty and integrity of India, the security, "strategic, scientific or economic" interests of the State, relation with foreign State or lead to incitement of an offense;
* Information which has been expressly forbidden to be published by any court of law or tribunal or the disclosure of which may constitute contempt of court;
* Information, the disclosure of which would cause a breach of privilege of Parliament or the State Legislature;
* Information including commercial confidence, trade secrets or intellectual property, the disclosure of which would harm the competitive position of a third party, unless the competent authority is satisfied that larger public interest warrants the disclosure of such information;
* Information available to a person in his fiduciary relationship, unless the competent authority is satisfied that the larger public interest warrants the disclosure of such information;
* Information received in confidence from foreign Government;
* Information, the disclosure of which would endanger the life or physical safety of any person or identify the source of information or assistance given in confidence for law enforcement or security purposes;
* Information which would impede the process of

investigation or apprehension or prosecution of offenders;

* Cabinet papers including records of deliberations of the Council of Ministers, Secretaries and other officers;
* Information which relates to personal information the disclosure of which has no relationship to any public activity or interest, or which would cause unwarranted invasion of the privacy of the individual (but it is also provided that the information which cannot be denied to the Parliament or a State Legislature shall not be denied by this exemption);
* Notwithstanding any of the exemptions listed above, a public authority may allow access to information, if public interest in disclosure outweighs the harm to the protected interests. (NB: This provision is qualified by the proviso to sub-section 11(1) of the Act which exempts disclosure of "trade or commercial secrets protected by law" under this clause when read along with 8(1)(d))

ROLE OF THE GOVERNMENT

Section 26 of the Act enjoins the central government, as also the state governments of the Union of India (excluding J&K), to initiate necessary steps to:

* Develop educational programs for the public especially disadvantaged communities on RTI.
* Encourage Public Authorities to participate in the development and organization of such programs.
* Promote timely dissemination of accurate information to the public.
* Train officers and develop training materials.
* Compile and disseminate a User Guide for the public

in the respective official language.

* Publish names, designation postal addresses and contact details of PIOs and other information such as notices regarding fees to be paid, remedies available in law if request is rejected etc.

POWER TO MAKE RULES

* The Central Government, State Governments and the Competent Authorities as defined in S.2(e) are vested with powers to make rules to carry out the provisions of the Right to Information Act, 2005. (S.27 & S.28)

RESIDUARY POWERS

* If any difficulty arises in giving effect to the provisions in the Act, the Central Government may, by Order published in the Official Gazette, make provisions necessary/expedient for removing the difficulty. (S.30)

EFFECTS

In the first year of National RTI, 42,876 (not yet official) applications for information were filed to Central (i.e. Federal) public authorities. Of these 878 were disputed at the final appellate stage - the Central Information Commission at New Delhi. A few of these decisions have thereafter been mired in further legal controversy in the various High Courts of India. The first stay order against a final appellate decision of the Central Information Commission was granted on 3.May.2006 by the High Court of Delhi in WP(C)6833-35/2006 cited as "NDPL & Ors. versus Central Information Commission & Ors". The Government of India's purported intention in 2006 to amend the RTI Act was postponed after public disquiet, but has been revived again in 2009 by the DoPT.

8

MAIN SUPPORTORS OF ANNA HAZARE

ARVIND KUMAR KEJRIWAL

Arvind Kumar Kejriwal (born 16 June 1968) is an Indian social activist fighting for greater transparency in Government. He was awarded Ramon Magsaysay Award for Emergent Leadership in 2006, for activating India's Right to Information movement at grassroots and social activities to empower the poorest citizens to fight corruption by holding the government answerable to the people. Kejriwal is also a Saathi (fellow) of the Association for India's Development.

Arvind Kejriwal was born in a Marwari family in Hissar, Haryana in 1968.His father was an engineer and he spent most of his childhood living in small northern Indian towns like Sonepat, Mathura and Hissar. Kejriwal graduated from IIT Kharagpur as a Mechanical engineer in 1989.

Kejriwal joined Tata Steel after his graduation from IIT Kharagpur. After quitting his job with Tata Steel, he spent some time working with Mother Teresa in Kolkata, the Ramakrishna Mission in the North-East India and Nehru Yuva Kendra.

Kejriwal joined the Indian Revenue Service (IRS) in 1995 and worked as an Additional Commissioner of Income Tax in Delhi. In January 2000, he took a sabbatical from work and founded Parivartan, a Delhi based citizens' movement which works on ensuring a just, transparent and accountable governance. Thereafter, in February 2006, he resigned from the job, to work full-time at Parivartan. In December 2006, Kejriwal along with Manish Sisodia and Abhinandan Sekhri started Public Cause Research Foundation, which works in promoting better local self governance and RTI related campaigns.

Right to Information

He along with Aruna Roy and others, campaigned for the Right to Information Act (RTI), which soon became a silent social movement, Delhi Right to Information Act was passed in 2001 and eventually at national level Indian Parliament passed the RTI in 2005. Thereafter, in July 2006, he spearheaded an awareness campaign for RTI across India. To motivate others Arvind has now instituted an RTI Award through his organisation. Kejriwal has been using RTI in corruption cases in many government departments including the Income Tax department, the Municipal Corporation of Delhi, the Public Distribution System (PDS), the Delhi Electricity Board and others.

As a member of India Against Corruption (IAC) Kejriwal is an active participant in the movement for the enactment of Jan Lokpal Bill. He is considered a key figure along with social activist Anna Hazare. On August 16 2011, key members of the India Against Corruption including Kejriwal were arrested, four hours before the planned indefinite hunger strike by Hazare. Rajan Bhagat, spokesman for Delhi Police, said police arrested Hazare under a legal provision that bans public gatherings and protests at the park in Delhi where Hazare was planning to begin his hunger strike. Activists were later released same day although they spent two more days in the Tihar jail negotiating conditions put on protest. Kejriwal left the jail on August 18 and the protests started the following day from Ramlila Maidan in Delhi. After twelve days of protests and many discussions between the government and the activists, Parliament passed a resolution to consider three points in drafting of Lokpal bill.

AWARDS

2004: Ashoka Fellow, Civic Engagement.

2005: 'Satyendra Dubey Memorial Award', IIT Kanpur for his campaign for bringing transparency in Government.

2006: Ramon Magsaysay Award for Eminent Leadership.

2006: CNN-IBN, 'Indian of the Year' in Public Service

2009: Distinguished Alumnus Award, IIT Kharagpur for Eminent Leadership.

2010: Policy Change Agent of the Year, The Economic Times Awards for Corporate Excellence along with Aruna Roy.

KIRAN BEDI

Kiran Bedi (born 9 June 1949) is an Indian social activist and a retired 1972 batch Indian Police Service officer. She held the post of Director General at the Bureau of Police Research and Development before she voluntary retired from the IPS in December 2007. She was the host and TV judge of the popular TV series "Aap Ki Kachehri" (English, "Your Court"), broadcast on the Indian TV channel, Star Plus. This program features Indian families approaching her TV court and explaining their problems to her. She then offers legal advice and monetary help to solve the problem. This program is classified as an EDUtainment program, as it attempts to simplify and explain legal procedures and Indian law to the viewers.

She has also founded two NGOs in India: Navjyoti for welfare and preventive policing in 1987 and the India Vision Foundation for prison reformation, drug abuse prevention and child welfare in 1994. She is one of the winners of the 2011 Bharatiya Manavata Vikas Puraskar.

SOCIAL INITIATIVES

Navjyoti (which literally means New Enlightenment), set up in 1987, and India Vision Foundation, set up in 1994, are the two major voluntary organizations established by her with the objectives of improving the condition of drug addicts and poor people. Her efforts have won national and international recognition, and her organizations were awarded the "Serge Soitiroff Memorial Award" for drug abuse prevention by the United Nations.

After retirement, Kiran Bedi launched a new website, www.saferindia.com, on January 3, 2007. The motto of this website is to help people whose complaints are not accepted by the local police. This project is undertaken by the non-profit, voluntary and non-government organization she founded, the India Vision Foundation.

LOKPAL MOVEMENT

Kiran Bedi is one of the prominent members of the Anna Hazare team which is on a nationwide protest against corruption and is urging the government to enact the Lokpal Bill and has conducted numerous protests and demonstrations throughout the country in the last year. Kiran Bedi has done enormous efforts for the feeling of what a true independence is and Jan Lokpal is the light towards it.

On Aug 16th 2011, Kiran Bedi courted arrest as part of the agitation called for by anti-graft activist Anna Hazare, of which Kiran Bedi is one of the front-line members. However, she was later released in the evening.

In the Indian Parliament MPs have moved "Privilage Motion against Kiran Bedi and Om Puri" who have allegedly mocked the parliamentarians during the Anna Hazare agitation.

MANISH SISODIA

Manish Sisodia (born 5 January 1972) is an Indian social activist, recognized for being a key member in the 2011 Indian anti-corruption movement. Formerly a news producer at Zee News, Manish is an active RTI activist. He is the co-founder of Kabir and with Arvind Kejriwal of Public Cause Research Foundation, NGOs aimed at creating awareness about Indian laws like the RTI.

SHANTI BHUSHAN

Shanti Bhushan (born 11 November 1925) is a former Law Minister of India at Ministry of Law and Justice (1977–1979) in the Morarji Desai Ministry and also a senior advocate. He along with his son Prashant Bhushan was featured at 74th position in a list of the most powerful

Indians published by The Indian Express in 2009.

Bhushan was an active member of Congress (O) party and later the Janata Party. He was a member of the Rajya Sabha from 14 July 1977 to 2 April 1980 and the Union Law minister in the Morarji Desai ministry from 1977 to 1979. He joined the Bhartiya Janata Party in 1980. In 1986, he resigned from BJP after the party acted against his advice over an election petition.

As the then Law Minister, he introduced the Lokpal bill in 1977. However, it did not pass because of the collapse of the government. He is presently co-chairman of the joint committee constituted in April 2011 for the Jan Lokpal Bill.

PRASHANT BHUSHAN

Prashant Bhushan (born 1956) is an Indian lawyer and social activist. He is the son of eminent lawyer Shanti Bhushan. He Lives in Noida.

He is an activist who helps people through the judiciary system. In his career of 15 years he has worked on around 500 PILs (Public interest Litigation). He is a strong supporter of a Clean Judiciary.

He is a member of the committee constituted in April 2011 for the Jan Lokpal bill.

He studied in IIT Madras, which he quit after a semester in Mechanical Engineering. He studied economics and then philosophy (of science) at Princeton.

SWAMI RAMDEV

Swami Ramdev, born as Ram Krishn Yadav on 11 January 1971, is popularly known as Baba Ramdev.

He was born in Seespaal Vihar(Alipur) of Mahendragarh district in Haryana state of India. According to the affidavit filed by him to the Passport Office his date of birth is 11 January 1971. He was inspired by the portraits of Ram Prasad Bismil and Subhas Chandra Bose that were hung in his room. According to his statements in an open Yog Shivir at Shahjahanpur (U.P.), when he grew up and read the autobiography of Ram Prasad Bismil, his mind was totally cleansed. After completing his middle education of eighth standard from Shahbajpur Haryana, he joined Aarsh (Arya) Gurukul, Khanpur and studied Sanskrit and Yoga under the guidance of Acharya Pradumn.

After he received teachings from Acharya Baldevji, he renounced worldly life, entering into Sanyas and changed his name from Ram Krishn to Ramdev.

In Kalva Gurukul of Jind district in Haryana India he offered free training of Yog to villagers for some time. Then he moved to Haridwar and spent several years studying ancient Indian scriptures at Gurukul Kangri Vishwavidyalaya. This included a rare book of Aurobindo Ghosh, *Yogik Sadhan*, translated from Bangla into Hindi by Pandit Ram Prasad Bismil. After reading this small booklet he went to the caves of Himalaya and practiced intense self-discipline and meditation. According to Sanjay Upadhyaya's book "Ramdev - Myth and Reality", Ramdev fell seriously ill in his childhood and through his recovery discovered his techniques of yoga and meditation.

SRI SRI RAVI SHANKAR

Ravi Shankar usually known as Sri Sri Ravi Shankar, born Ravi Shankar Ratnam, born 13 May 1956) is a spiritual leader and founder of the Art of Living Foundation (founded 1982), which aims at relieving both individual stress and societal problems and violence. It is an NGO with UNESCO consultative status. He is also frequently referred to simply as "Sri Sri" (honorific) or as Guruji or Gurudev. He also established in 1997 a Geneva-based charity, along with the 14th Dalai Lama, the International Association for Human Values, an NGO that engages in relief work and rural development and aims to foster shared global values. In 2010 Shankar was named by Forbes Magazine as the fifth most influential person in India.

Shankar says that every emotion has a corresponding rhythm in the breath and regulating breath could help relieve personal suffering. After realizing Sudarshan Kriya, Shankar started sharing it with others through the Art of Living course, first held in Shimoga.

Shankar inspired his father and several other prominent citizens of Bangalore to find *Ved Vignan Maha Vidya Peeth*, an educational and charitable trust, in 1981. Under the auspices of this trust, he opened a school south of Bangalore for local rural children which now provides free education for 2,000 such children.

In 1983 Shankar held the first Art of Living course in Europe in Switzerland. In 1986 he travelled to Apple Valley, California in the USA to conduct the first course to be held in North America.

DR. KUMAR VISHWAS

Dr. Kumar Vishwas is a Hindi Poet. Kumar Vishwas was born on 10 February,1970 in Pilkhuwa, Ghaziabad, Uttar Pradesh. He is the youngest among four brothers and a sister. He started his schooling at Lala Ganga Sahay School, Pilkhuwa where he spent part of his childhood. His father, Dr. Chandra Pal Sharma, was a lecturer at R.S.S. Degree College, Pilkhuwa affiliated to Chaudhary Charan Singh University, Meerut. His mother Smt. Rama Sharma is a home maker. After completing his intermediate from Rajputana Regiment Inter College, Pilkhuwa, his father wanted him to be an engineer, but he had a passion for Poetry right from childhood. He took no interest in engineering and decided to make a career in the field of poetry. He did post graduation in Hindustani Literature. Vishvas started his career as a professor in the year 1994 from Rajasthan. He has been teaching Hindi Literature to higher class students for last sixteen years.

MEDHA PATKAR

Medha Patkar was born in Mumbai, Maharashtra to Indu and Vasant Khanolkar, a trade union leader and freedom fighter. She was raised by politically and socially active parents. Her father actively fought in the Indian Independence Movement. Her mother was a member of Swadar, an organization setup to help and assist women suffering difficult circumstances arising out of financial, educational, and health related problems. Her parents' activism played a role in shaping her philosophical views. She often known for her extreme views on growth of country and liberalization.

She did her M.A. in Social Work from Tata Institute of Social Sciences.

Author Jacques Leslie devoted a third of his book, *Deep Water: The Epic Struggle Over Dams, Displaced People, and the Environment* (Farrar, Straus & Giroux, 2005), to a portrait of Patkar as she planned to drown herself in rising reservoir waters behind the Sardar Sarovar Dam, whose construction she fought for two decades.

Medha Patkar is one of the recipients of Right Livelihood Award for the year 1991. She received the 1999 M.A. Thomas National Human Rights Award from Vigil India Movement. She has also received numerous other awards, including the Deena Nath Mangeshkar Award, Mahatma Phule Award, Goldman Environment Prize, Green Ribbon Award for Best International Political Campaigner by BBC, and the Human Rights Defender's Award from Amnesty International. She was also a Commissioner to the World Commission on Dams.

9
What is Jan Lokpal Bill?

BACKGROUND

The Lokpal bill was first introduced by Shanti Bhushan in 1968 and passed the 4th Lok Sabha (lower house) in 1969. But the Lok Sabha was dissolved before the bill got through the Rajya Sabha (upper house of the Parliament of India). The Subsequent versions were re-introduced in 1971, 1977, 1985, 1989, 1996, 1998, 2001, 2005 and in 2008, but none of them passed. The bill is inspired of setting up an independent commission like Independent Commission Against Corruption (Hong Kong) (ICAC).

Renewed calls for the bill arose over resentment of the major differences between the draft 2010 Lokpal Bill prepared by the government and that prepared by the members of the associated activists movement – N. Santosh Hegde, a former justice of the Supreme Court of India; Lokayukta of Karnataka; Shanti Bhushan; Arvind Kejriwal; Prashant Bhushan, a senior lawyer in the Supreme Court; and members of the India Against Corruption Movement.

The bill's supporters consider existing laws too weak, full of contradictions and insufficiently empowered to combat corruption. On the other hand, critics of the Jan Lokpal Bill argue that the bill attempts to supersede existing constitutional bodies and attempts to create a super-institution with sweeping powers, which can be dangerous for the future of democracy.

Key features of proposed bill

Some important features of the proposed bill are:

- To establish a central government anti-corruption institution called Lokpal, supported by Lokayukta at the state level.
- As in the case of the Supreme Court and Cabinet Secretariat, the Lokpal will be supervised by the Cabinet Secretary and the Election Commission. As a result, it will be completely independent of the government and free from ministerial influence in its investigations.
- Members will be appointed by judges, Indian Administrative Service officers with a clean record, private citizens and constitutional authorities through a transparent and participatory process.
- A selection committee will invite short-listed candidates for interviews, videorecordings of which will thereafter be made public.
- Every month on its website, the Lokayukta will publish a list of cases dealt with, brief details of each, their outcome and any action taken or proposed. It will also publish lists of all cases received by the Lokayukta during the previous month, cases dealt with and those which are pending.
- Investigations of each case must be completed in one year. Any resulting trials should be concluded in the following year, giving a total maximum process time of two years.
- Losses caused to the government by a corrupt individual will be recovered at the time of conviction.

- Government officework required by a citizen that is not completed within a prescribed time period will result in Lokpal imposing financial penalties on those responsible, which will then be given as compensation to the complainant.
- Complaints against any officer of Lokpal will be investigated and completed within a month and, if found to be substantive, will result in the officer being dismissed within two months.
- The existing anti-corruption agencies (CVC, departmental vigilance and the anti-corruption branch of the CBI) will be merged into Lokpal which will have complete power and authority to independently investigate and prosecute any officer, judge or politician.
- Whistleblowers who alert the agency to potential corruption cases will also be provided with protection by it.

Difference between Draft Lokpal Bill and Jan Lokpal Bill

HIGHLIGHTS

Jan Lokpal Bill (Citizen's Ombudsman Bill)	Draft Lokpal Bill (2010)
Lokpal will have powers to initiate suo moto action or receive complaints of corruption from the general public.	Lokpal will have no power to initiate suo motu action or receive complaints of corruption from the general public. It can only probe complaints forwarded by the Speaker of the Lok Sabha or the Chairman of the Rajya Sabha.
Lokpal will have the power to initiate prosecution of anyone found guilty.	Lokpal will only be an Advisory Body with a role limited to forwarding reports to a "Competent Authority".

Lokpal will have police powers as well as the ability to register FIRs.	Lokpal will have no police powers and no ability to register an FIR or proceed with criminal investigations.
Lokpal and the anti corruption wing of the CBI will be one independent body.	The CBI and Lokpal will be unconnected.
Punishments will be a minimum of 10 years and a maximum of up to life imprisonment.	Punishment for corruption will be a minimum of 6 months and a maximum of up to 7 years.

DETAILED

The following table details differences between the Government and activist backed versions

Issue	The Jan Lokpal Bill	Government's Lokpal Bill
Prime Minister	Can be investigated with permission of seven member Lokpal bench.	PM can be investigated by Lokpal after she/he vacates office.
Judiciary	Can be investigated, though high level members may be investigated only with permission of a seven member Lokpal bench.	Judiciary is exempt and will be covered by a separate "judicial accountability bill".
Conduct of MPs	Can be investigated with permission of seven member Lokpal bench.	Can be investigated, but their conduct within Parliament, such as voting, cannot be investigated.
Lower bureaucracy	All public servants would be included.	Only senior officers (Group A) will be covered.

Anti-corruption wing of the Central Bureau of Investigation (CBI)	The Anti-corruption wing of the CBI will be merged into the Lokpal.	The Anti-corruption wing of the CBI not be merged into the Lokpal.
Removal of Lokpal members and Chair	Any person can bring a complaint to the Supreme Court, who can then recommend removal of any member to the President.	Any "aggrieved party" can raise a complaint to the President, who will refer the matter to the CJI.
Removal of Lokpal staff and officers	Complaints against Lokpal staff will be handled by independent boards set-up in each state, composed of retired bureaucrats, judges, and civil society members.	Lokpal will conduct inquiries into its own behavior.
Lokayukta	Lokakyukta and other local/state anti-corruption agency would remain in place.	All state anti-corruption agencies would be closed and responsibilities taken over by centralized Lokpal.
Whistleblower protection	Whistleblowers are protected by Lokpal.	No protection granted to whistleblowers by Lokpal.
Punishment for corruption	Lokpal can either directly impose penalties, or refer the matter to the courts. Penalties can include removal from office, imprisonment, and recovery of assets from those who benefited from the corruption.	Lokpal can only refer matters to the courts, not take any direct punitive actions. Penalties remain equivalent to those in current law.

Investigatory powers	Lokpal can obtain wiretaps (to make a connection to a telegraph or telephone wire in order to obtain information secretly), issue rogatory letters, and recruit investigating officers. Cannot issue contempt orders.	Lokpal can issue contempt orders, and has the ability to punish those in contempt. No authority to obtain wiretaps, issue rogatory letters, or recruit investigating officers.
False, frivolous and vexatious complaints	Lokpal can issue fines for frivolous complaints (including frivolous complaints against Lokpal itself), with a maximum penalty of Rs 1 lakh.	Court system will handle matters of frivolous complaints. Courts can give 2-5 years imprisonment and fines of Rs 25,000 to 2 lakh.
NGOs	NGOs not within the scope due to their role in exposing corruption.	NGOs are within the scope and can be investigated.

Campaign for the Jan Lokpal Bill

The first version of the Lokpal Bill drafted by the Government of India in 2010 was considered ineffective by anti-corruption activists from the civil society. These activists, under the banner of India Against Corruption, came together to draft a citizen's version of the Lokpal Bill later called the Jan Lokpal. Public awareness drives and protest marches were carried out to campaign for the bill. However, public support for the Jan Lokpal Bill draft started gathering steam after Anna Hazare, a noted Gandhian announced that he would hold an indefinite fast from April 5, 2011 for the passing of the Lokpal/Jan Lokpal bill.

To dissuade Hazare from going on an indefinite hunger

strike, the Prime Minister's Office directed the ministries of personnel and law to examine how the views of society activists can be included in the Lokpal Bill. On April 5, the National Advisory Council rejected the Lokpal bill drafted by the government. Union Human Resource Development Minister Kapil Sibal then met social activists Swami Agnivesh and Arvind Kejriwal on 7 April to find ways to bridge differences over the bill. However, no consensus could be reached on April 7 owing to several differences of opinion between the social activists and the Government.

Fast & Agitation–Phase 1

On April 7, Anna Hazare called for a *Jail Bharo Andolan* (fill jail movement) from April 13 to protest against Government's rejection of their demands. Anna Hazare also claimed that his group has received six crore (60 million) text messages of support and that he had further backing from a large number of Internet activists. The outpouring of support was largely free of political overtones; political parties were specifically discouraged from participating in the movement. The fast ended on April 9, after 98 hours, when the Government accepted most demands due to public pressure. Anna Hazare set an August 15 deadline for the passing of the bill in the Parliament, failing which he would start a hunger strike from August 16. The fast also led to the Government of India agreeing to setting up a Joint Drafting Committee, which would complete its work by June 30.

Drafting Committee

The drafting committee was officially formed on 8 April 2011. It consisted of the following ten members, including five from the government and five drawn from the civil society

Member	Qualifications and status
Pranab Mukherjee	Finance Minister, Co-Chairman
Shanti Bhushan	Former Minister of Law and Justice, Co-Chairman
P. Chidambaram	Minister of Home Affairs
Veerappa Moily	Minister of Corporate Affairs
Kapil Sibal	Minister for Communications and Information Technology
Salman Khursid	Minister of Law
Anna Hazare	Social Activist
Prashant Bhushan	Lawyer
N. Santosh Hegde	Former Lokayukta (Karnataka) and
Arvind Kejriwal	RTI Activist.

The Government's handling of the formation of the draft committee, involving the civil society in preparation of the draft Lokpal bill, was criticized by various political parties including BJP, BJD, TDP,AIADMK, CPI-M, RJD, JD(U) and Samajwadi Party.

The committee failed to agree on the terms of a compromise bill and the government introduced its own version of the bill in the parliament in August 2011.

Fast & Agitation–Phase 2

However, the Joint Drafting Committee failed to reach a conclusion and the five members of the Government on the panel came up with their own version of the bill, which was considered by Anna and his team as weak and will facilitate the corrupt to go free apart from several other differences. To protest against this, Anna Hazare announced an "Indefinite Fast". Anna and his team asked for permission from Delhi Police for their fast and agitation at Jantar Mantar or JP Park. Delhi Police gave its permission with certain conditions. These condition were considered by team Anna as restrictive and against the fundamental constitutional rights and they decided to defy the conditions. Delhi Police imposed sec 144 CrPC.

On Aug 16, Anna Hazare was taken into preventive custody by Delhi Police. Senior officers of Delhi Police reached Anna Hazare's flat early in the morning and informed him that he could not leave his home. However, Hazare turned down the request following which he was detained.Anna in his recorded address to the nation before his arrest asked his supporters not to stop the agitation and urged the protesters to remain peaceful.Other members of "India Against Corruption", Arvind Kejriwal, Kiran Bedi and Manish Sisodia were also taken into preventive custody. Kiran Bedi described the situation as resembling a kind of Emergency (referring to the Emergency imposed in 1975 by the Indira Gandhi Govt.).

The arrest resulted in huge public outcry and under pressure the government released him in the evening of Aug 16. However, Anna Hazare refused to come out of Jail, starting his indefinite fast from Jail itself. Manish Sisodia explained his situation as, "Anna said that he left home to go to JP Park to conduct his fast and that is exactly where he would go from here (Tihar Jail). He has refused to be released till he is given a written, unconditional permission". Unwilling to use forces owing to the sensitive nature of the case, the jail authorities had no option but to let Anna spend the night inside Tihar. Later on 17th Aug, Delhi Police permitted Anna Hazare and team to use the Ramlila Maidan for the proposed fast and agitation withdrawing most of the contentious provisions they had imposed earlier. The indefinite fast and agitation began in

Ramlila Maidan, New Delhi, and was on till August 28, 2011 for 13 days. He broke his fast at 10.20 a.m. by drinking a glass of coconut water with honey offered to him by two girls, Ikra and Simran.

Notable supporters and opposition

In addition to the activists responsible for creating and organizing support for the bill, a wide variety of other notable individuals have also stated that they support this bill. Spiritual leaders Sri Sri Ravi Shankar and Yog Guru Ramdev expressed support. Notable politicians who indicated support for the bill include Ajit Singh and Manpreet Singh Badal as well as the principal opposition party, Bharatiya Janta Party. In addition, numerous Bollywood actors, directors, and musicians publicly approved of the bill.

Notable opposition to the activists' version of the Bill was expressed by HRD minister Kapil Sibal and other Congress leaders; Chief Minister of West Bengal Mamta Banerjee; Punjab Chief Minister and Akali Dal leader Prakash Singh Badal; Shiv Sena leader Bal Thackeray, and former Chief Justice of the Supreme Court Jagdish Sharan Verma. Although BJP showed their support earlier, there were reports that BJP shared Congress's concern "over letting the civil society gain the upper hand over Parliament in lawmaking".

Criticisms of the bill

The bill has been criticized as being naïve in its approach to combating corruption. According to Pratap Bhanu Mehta, President of the Center for Policy Research Delhi writes that the bill "is premised on an institutional imagination that is at best naïve; at worst subversive of representative democracy". The very concept of a Lokpal concept has received criticism from HRD minister Kapil Sibal in that it will lack accountability, be oppresive and undemocratic.

Extra-constitutional

The pro-bill activist Arvind Kejriwal rejects the claim of Lokpal being extra-constitutional with the explanation that the body will only investigate corruption offences and submit a charge sheet which would then tried and prosecuted through trial courts and higher courts. And that other bodies with equivalent powers in other matters exist. And also that the proposed bill also lists clear provisions for the Supreme Court to abolish the Lokpal.

Despite these clarifications, critics feel that the exact judicial powers of LokPal are rather unclear in comparison with its investigative powers. The bill requires "...members of Lokpal and the officers in investigation wing of Lokpal shall be deemed to be police officers". Although some supporters have denied any judicial powers of Lokpal, the government and some critics have recognized Lokpal to have quasi-judicial powers.

The bill also states that "Lokpal shall have, and exercise the same jurisdiction powers and authority in respect of contempt of itself as a High court has and may exercise, and, for this purpose, the provisions of the Contempt of Courts Act, 1971 (Central Act 70 of 1971) shall have the effect subject to the modification that the references therein to the High Court shall be construed as including a reference to the Lokpal." Review of proceedings and decisions by Lokpal is prevented in the bill by the statement "...no proceedings or decision of the Lokpal shall be liable to be challenged, reviewed, quashed or called in question in any court of ordinary Civil Jurisdiction.". As a result, how the trials will be conducted is unclear in the bill, although the bill outlines requiring judges for special courts, presumably to conduct trial that should be completed within one year. The critics hence express concern that, without judicial review, Lokpal could potentially become an extra-constitutional body with investigative and judicial powers whose decisions cannot be reviewed in regular courts.

Legislator support

Post the massive support to Anna Hazare's movement, several of the MPs across party lines have come out in support to the Jan Lokpal Bill. Most notable names are Congress MPs from Maharashtra Priya Dutt and Datta Meghe. Datta Meghe also demanded that his party spokesperson Manish Tiwari should apologize to Anna Hazare for his uncharitable comments.

This support started coming as over 150 MPs and Ministers from different states were forced to remain confined to their houses as Anna supporters protested outside their houses. Protests were also seen outside the residence of Sheila Dixit CM of Delhi, Kapil Sibal, Pranab Mukherjee amongst others.

BJP MP Varun Gandhi tried to introduce Jan Lokpal Bill as a private member's bill in the parliament.

Social media

As per the reports, Anna Hazare's fast was successful in mobilizing the support of thousands in the virtual world of social media. On Independence Day, Anna had over five lakh mentions through status updates and comments across top social networking sites, including Facebook and Twitter in the country. Two days later, the number had shot up to 9 million.On YouTube, over 40,000 people watched the video shot by Kiran Bedi inside Tihar Jail in which Anna has addressed his supporters. Facebook has 542 fan pages by Anna's name.

Online surveys

According to the survey conducted by STAR News and Nielsen, 87% of the 8900 respondents of the survey supported the Jan Lokpal Bill. The survey–conducted in 28 cities across the country, including all four metros–mainly deals with three important points: public's knowledge about the Lokpal Bill; awareness about Anna's campaign; and the perceived problems with the Jan Lokpal Bill.

Over a million people joined the Times of India online anti-graft campaign, in one of the biggest ever voting exercises in the virtual world. The news analysis points that citizens want to make their voices heard and have found the platform offered by the campaign a viable one to do so.

SUPPORT FROM FILM PERSONALITIES

Some of the actors, directors, and film personalities who openly supported Anna Hazare: Amir Khan, Rajkumar Hirani, Sonu Nigam, Kailash Kher, Manoj Twari, Om Puri, Ashok Pandit, Sumbhavana Seth, A. R. Rehman, Anupam Kher, Bipasha Basu, Alka Yagnik, Shabana Azmi, Manisha Lamba, Shekhar & Vishal Dadlani, R. Madhavan, Atul Kasbekar, Anurag Kashyap, Milind Sonam and many more.

10

Government of India Draft Lokpal Bill

THE LOKPAL BILL, 2011

ARRANGEMENT OF CLAUSES

CHAPTER I

PRELIMINARY

1. Short title and commencement.
2. Definitions.

CHAPTER II

ESTABLISHMENT OF LOKPAL

3. Establishment of Lokpal.
4. Appointment of chairperson and other Members and Selection Committee.
5. Filling of vacancies of Chairperson or other Members.
6. Term of office and other conditions of service of Chairperson and Members.
7. Salary, allowances and other conditions of service of Chairperson and Members.
8. Removal and suspension of Chairperson and other Member of Lokpal.
9. Restriction on employment by Chairperson and Members after ceasing to hold office.
10. Member to act as Chairperson or to discharge his functions in certain circumstances.
11. Secretary, other Officers and staff of Lokpal.

CHAPTER III

INVESTIGATION WING

12. Investigation Wing.
13. Investigation officer to have powers of police.

14. Investigation officer to inquire on direction of Lokpal.

CHAPTER IV
PROSECUTION WING

15. Appointment of Prosecution Director.

CHAPTER V
EXPENSES OF INSTITUTION OF LOKPAL TO BE CHARGED ON CONSOLIDATED FUND OF INDIA

16. Expenses of Lokpal to be charged on Consolidated Fund of India.

CHAPTER VI
JURISDICTION IN RESPECT OF INQUIRY

17. Jurisdiction of Lokpal.
18. Matters pending before any court or committee or authority before inquiry before Lokpal not to be affected.
19. Constitution of benches of Lokpal.
20. Distribution of business amongst Benches
21. Power of Chairperson to transfer cases
22. Decision to be by majority.

CHAPTER VII
PROCEDURE IN RESPECT OF INQUIRY AND INVESTIGATION

23. Provisions relating to complaints and inquiry and investigation.
24. Persons likely to be prejudicially affected to be heard.
25. Lokpal may require any public servant or any other person to furnish information, etc.
26. Previous sanction not necessary for investigation and initiating prosecution by Lokpal in certain cases.
27. Action on inquiry in relation to public servants not being minsters or Members of Parliament.
28. Action on inquiry against public servant being ministers or Members of Parliament.

CHAPTER VIII
POWERS OF LOKPAL

29. Search and seizure.
30. Lokpal to have powers of civil court in certain cases.
31. Power to punish for contempt.
32. Power of Lokpal to utilise services of officers of Central or State Government.

33. Provisional attachment of assets.
34. Confirmation of attachment of assets.
35. Power of Lokpal to recommend discontinuance of activity connected with allegation of corruption.
36. Power of Lokpal to give directions to prevent destruction of records during inquiry.
37. Power to delegate.

CHAPTER IX

SPECIAL COURTS

38. Special Courts to be notified by Central Government.
39. Letter of request to a contracting State in certain cases.

CHAPTER X

COMPLAINTS AGAINST CHAIRPERSON, MEMBERS AND OFFICIALS OF LOKPAL

40. Complaints against Chairperson and Members not to be inquired by Lokpal.
41. Complaints against officials of Lokpal.

CHAPTER XI

ASSESSMENT OF LOSS AND RECOVERY THEREOF BY SPECIAL COURT

42. Assessment of loss and recovery thereof by Special Court.

CHAPTER XII

FINANCE, ACCOUNTS AND AUDIT

43. Budget.
44. Grants by Central Government.
45. Annual statement of accounts.
46. Furnishing of returns, etc., to Central Government.

CHAPTER XIII

DECLARATION OF ASSETS

47. Declaration of assets.
48. Presumption as to acquisition of assets by corrupt means in certain cases.

CHAPTER XIV

CITIZENS' CHARTER

49. Citizens' charter.

CHAPTER XV

OFFENCES AND PENALTIES

50. Prosecution for false complaint and payment of compensation, etc., to public servant.

THE LOKPAL BILL, 2011
A
BILL

to provide for the establishment of the institution of Lokpal to inquire into allegations of corruption against certain public functionaries and for matters connected therewith.

WHEREAS the Constitution of India established a democratic Republic to ensure justice for all;

AND WHEREAS good governance is the bedrock of democracy and the guarantee of development as a right of the citizen;

AND WHEREAS Parliament has progressively and incrementally contributed to the body of law to fulfil the aspirations of the citizens of India;

AND WHEREAS various institutions of governance as well as democratic institutions have worked to strengthen participatory democracy;

AND WHEREAS the rapid growth of democratic and economic institutions have brought new challenges of accountability and integrity in the course of governance;

AND WHEREAS graft and corruption have become a serious menace to society and governance;

AND WHEREAS serious concerns have been expressed about the grave consequences of corruption in high places;

AND WHEREAS India is a signatory to the United Nations Convention Against Corruption;

AND WHEREAS the country's commitment to clean and responsive governance has to be reflected in an effective institution to contain and punish acts of corruption;

NOW, THEREFORE, it is expedient to provide for prompt and fair investigation and prosecution of cases of corruption.

BE it enacted by Parliament in the Sixty-second Year of the Republic of India as follows:–

CHAPTER I
PRELIMINARY

1. Short title and commencement.

(1) This Act may be called the Lokpal Act, 2011.

(2) It shall come into force on such date as the Central Government may, by notification in the Official Gazette, appoint; and different dates may be appointed for different

provisions of this Act and any reference in any provision to the commencement of this Act shall be construed as reference to the coming into force of that provision..

2. **Definitions.**

(1) In this Act, unless the context otherwise requires,–

(a) "Bench" means a Bench of the Lokpal;

(b) "Chairperson" means the Chairperson of the Lokpal;

(c) "Competent authority", in relation to–

(i) a member of the Council of Ministers, means the Prime Minister;

(ii) a member of Parliament other than a Minister means the Council of States in the case of a member of that Council and the House of the People in the case of a member of that House;

(iii) an officer in the Ministry or Department of the Central Government means the Minister in charge of the Ministry or Department under which such officer is serving;

(iv) a chairperson or members of any body, or Board or corporation or authority or company or society or autonomous body (by whatever name called) established or constituted under an Act of Parliament or wholly or partly financed by the Central Government or controlled by it means the Minister in charge of the administrative Ministry of such body, or Board or corporation or authority or company or society or autonomous body;

(v) an officer of any body or Board or corporation or authority or company or society or autonomous body (by whatever name called) established or constituted under an Act of Parliament or wholly or partly financed by the Central Government or controlled by it means the head of such body or Board or corporation or authority or company or society or autonomous body;

(d) "complaint" means a complaint alleging that a public servant has committed an offence punishable under the Prevention of Corruption Act, 1988; (49 of 1988)

(e) "inquiry" means every inquiry conducted under this Act by the Lokpal;

(f) "Judicial Member" means a Judicial Member of the Lokpal appointed as such;

(g) "Lokpal" means the institution established under section 3;

(h) "Member" means a Member of the Lokpal;

(i) "Minister" means an Union Minister but does not include the Prime Minister;

(j) "notification" means notification published in the Official Gazette and the expression "notify" shall be construed accordingly;

(k) "prescribed" means prescribed by rules made under this Act;

(l) "public servant" means a person referred to in clauses (a) to (e) of sub-section (1) of section 17;

(m) "regulations" means regulations made under this Act;

(n) "Schedule" means a Schedule to this Act;

(o) "Special Court" means a Special Court appointed under sub-section (1) of section 3 of the Prevention of Corruption Act, 1988.

(2) Words and expressions used herein and not defined in this Act but defined in the Prevention of Corruption Act, 1988, shall have the meanings respectively assigned to them in that Act.

CHAPTER II
ESTABLISHMENT OF LOKPAL

3. **Establishment of Lokpal**

(1) As from the commencement of this Act, there shall be established, for the purpose of making inquiries in respect of complaints made under this Act, an institution to be called the "Lokpal".

(2) The Lokpal shall consist of–

(a) a Chairperson; and

(b) ten Members, out of whom at least four shall be Judicial Members.

(3) A person shall be eligible to be appointed,–

(a) as the Chairperson or a Member if he is a person of impeccable integrity, outstanding ability and standing having special knowledge of, and professional experience of not less than twenty-five years in, public affairs, administrative law and policy, academics, commerce and industry, law, finance or management;

(b) as a Judicial Member if he is or has been a Chief Justice of a High Court or a Judge of the Supreme Court.

(4) The Chairperson or a Member shall not be a member of Parliament or a member of the Legislature of any State or Union territory and shall not hold any office of trust or profit (other than his office as the Chairperson or a Member) or be connected with any political party or carry on any business or practise any profession and accordingly, before he enters upon his office, a person appointed as the Chairperson or a Member, as the case may be, shall, if -

(a) he is a member of Parliament or of the Legislature of any State or Union territory, resign from such membership; or

(b) he holds any office of trust or profit, resign from such office; or

(c) he is connected with any political party, sever his connection with it; or

(d) he is carrying on any business, sever his connection with the conduct and management of such business; or

(e) he is practicing any profession, cease to practise such profession.

(5) The Chairperson and every Member shall, before entering upon his office, make and subscribe before the President an oath or affirmation in the form set out in the First Schedule.

4. **Appointment of Chairperson and other Members and Selection Committee.**

(1) The Chairperson and Members shall be appointed by the President after obtaining the recommendations of a Selection Committee consisting of–

(a) the Prime Minister – chairperson;

(b) the Speaker of the House of the People –member;

(c) the Leader of the House other than the House in which the Prime Minister is a Member of Parliament –member;

(d) the Minister in-charge of the Ministry of Home Affairs in the Government of India –member;

(e) the Leader of the Opposition in the House of the People– member;

(f) the Leader of the Opposition in the Council of States – member:

Provided that in case, there is no Leader of Opposition in the House of the People or the Council of States, the leader of the single largest group or party in opposition to the Government, as the case may be, in such House or Council shall be deemed to be a member of the Committee specified in clause (e) or clause (f), as the case may be:

(g) one sitting Judge of the Supreme Court to be nominated by the Chief Justice of India–member;

(h) one sitting Chief Justice of a High Court to be nominated by the Chief Justice of India–member;

(i) the President of the National Academy of Sciences, India, being a society registered under the Societies Registration Act, 1860 or the senior most National Professor – member; (21 of 1860)

(j) Cabinet Secretary–secretary.

(2) No appointment of a Chairperson or a Member shall be invalid merely by reason of any vacancy in the Committee.

(3) The Selection Committee may, if it considers necessary for the purposes of selecting the Chairperson and other members of the Lokpal and for preparing a panel of persons to be considered for appointment as such, constitute a Search Committee consisting of such persons of impeccable integrity and outstanding ability and standing having special knowledge of, and professional experience of not less than twenty-five years in, public affairs, administrative law and policy, academics, commerce and industry, law, finance, management, or in any other matter which in

the opinion of the Selection Committee, may be useful in making selection of Chairperson and other Members of the Lokpal.

(4) The Selection Committee shall regulate its own procedure for selecting the Chairperson and Members of the Lokpal which shall be transparent.

(5) The term of the search committee referred to in sub-section (3) and fee and allowances payable to the members of the search committee and the manner of selection of panel of names shall be such as may be prescribed.

5. **Filling of vacancies of Chairperson or other Members.**

The President shall take or cause to be taken all necessary steps for the appointment of a new Chairperson and other Members at least three months before the expiry of the term of such Chairperson or Member, as the case may be, in accordance with the procedure laid down in this Act.

6. **Term of office of Chairperson and Members.**

The Chairperson and every other Member shall, on the recommendations of the Selection Committee, be appointed by the President by warrant under his hand and seal and hold office as such for a term not exceeding five years from the date on which he enters upon his office or until he attains the age of seventy years, whichever is earlier:

Provided that he may–

(a) by writing under his hand addressed to the President, resign his office; or

(b) be removed from his office in the manner provided in section 8.

7. **Salary, allowances and other conditions of service of Chairperson and Members.**

The salary, allowances and other conditions of service of–

(i) the Chairperson shall be the same as those of the Chief Justice of India;

(ii) other Members shall be the same as those of a Judge of the Supreme Court:

Provided that if the Chairperson or a Member is, at the time of his appointment, in receipt of pension (other than disability pension) in respect of any previous service under the Government of India or under the Government of a State, his salary in respect of service as the Chairperson or, as the case may be, as a Member, be reduced–

(a) by the amount of that pension; and

(b) if he has, before such appointment, received, in lieu of a portion of the pension due to him in respect of such previous service, the commuted value thereof, by the amount of that portion of the pension:

Provided further that the salary, allowances and pension payable to, and other conditions of service of, the Chairperson or a Member shall not be varied to his disadvantage after his appointment.

8. **Removal and suspension of Chairperson and other Member of Lokpal.**

(1) Subject to the provisions of sub-section (3), the Chairperson or any other Member shall be removed from his office by order of the President on grounds of misbehaviour after the Supreme Court, on a reference being made to it by the President, has, on inquiry held in accordance with the procedure prescribed in that behalf, reported that the Chairperson or such other Member, as the case may be, ought on any such ground to be removed.

(2) The President may suspend from office the Chairperson or any other Member in respect of whom a reference has been made to the Supreme Court under sub-section (1) until the President has passed orders on receipt of the report of the Supreme Court on such reference.

(3) Notwithstanding anything contained in sub-section (1), the President may by order remove from the office the Chairperson or any other Member if the Chairperson or such other Member, as the case may be,–

(a) is adjudged an insolvent; or

(b) engages during his term of office in any paid employment outside the duties of his office; or

(c) is, in the opinion of the President, unfit to continue in office by reason of infirmity of mind or body.

(4) If the Chairperson or any other Member is or becomes in any way concerned or interested in any contract or

agreement made by or on behalf of the Government of India or the Government of a State or participates in any way in the profit thereof or in any benefit or emolument arising therefrom otherwise than as a member and in common with the other members of an incorporated company, he shall, for the purposes of sub-section (1), be deemed to be guilty of misbehaviour.

9. **Restriction on employment by Chairperson and Members after ceasing to hold office.**

(1) On ceasing to hold office, the Chairperson and every other Member shall be ineligible for–

(i) re-appointment as the Chairperson or a Member of the Lokpal;

(ii) any diplomatic assignment, appointment as administrator of a Union territory and such other assignment or appointment which is required by law to be made by the President by warrant under his hand and seal;

(iii) further employment to any other office of profit under the Government of India or the Government of a State;

(iv) contesting any election of President or Vice President or Member of either House of Parliament or Member of either House of State Legislature or Municipality or Panchayat.

(2) Notwithstanding anything contained in sub-section (1), a Member shall be eligible to be appointed as a Chairperson, if his total tenure as Member and Chairperson does not exceed five years.

10. **Member to act as Chairperson or to discharge his functions in certain circumstances.**

(1) In the event of the occurrence of any vacancy in the office of Chairperson by reason of his death, resignation or otherwise, the President may, by notification, authorise the senior-most Member to act as the Chairperson until the appointment of a new Chairperson to fill such vacancy.

(2) When the Chairperson is unable to discharge his functions owing to absence on leave or otherwise, the senior-most Member available, as the President may, by notification,

authorise in this behalf, shall discharge the functions of the Chairperson until the date on which the Chairperson resumes his duties.

11. **Secretary, other Officers and staff of Lokpal.**

(1) The appointment of secretary and other officers and staff of the Lokpal shall be made by the Chairperson or such other Member or officer of Lokpal as the Chairperson may direct:

Provided that the President may by rule require that the appointment in respect of any post or posts as may be specified in the rule, shall be made after consultation with the Union Public Service Commission.

(2) Subject to the provisions of any law made by Parliament, the conditions of service of secretary and other officers and staff of the Lokpal shall be such as may be specified by regulations made by the Lokpal for the purpose:

Provided that the regulations made under this sub-section shall, so far as they relate to salaries, allowances, leave or pensions, require the approval of the President.

CHAPTER III
INVESTIGATION WING

12. **Investigation Wing.**

Notwithstanding anything contained in any law for the time being in force, the Lokpal shall constitute an Investigation Wing for the purpose of conducting investigation of any offence alleged to have been committed by a public servant punishable under the Prevention of Corruption Act, 1988: (49 of 1988)

Provided that till such time the Investigation Wing is constituted by the Lokpal, the Central Government shall make available such number of investigation officers and other staff from such of its Ministries or Departments, as may be required by the Lokpal, for carrying out investigation under this Act.

13. **Investigation officer to have powers of police.**

(1) No investigation shall be made by an investigation officer of the Investigation Wing below the rank of a Deputy Superintendent of Police or by any other officer of equivalent rank.

(2) The investigation officers of the Investigation Wing shall have in relation to the investigation of such offences, all the powers, duties, privileges and liabilities which police officers have in connection with the investigation of such offences.

14. Investigation officer to inquire on direction of Lokpal

(1) The Lokpal may, before holding any inquiry under this Act, by an order, require the investigation officer of its Investigation Wing to make, or cause to be made, a preliminary investigation in such manner as it may direct and submit a report to the Lokpal, within such time as may be specified by the Lokpal, to enable it to satisfy itself as to whether or not the matter requires to be inquired into by the Lokpal.

(2) The investigation officer on receipt of an order under sub-section (1) shall complete the investigation and submit his report within the time specified under that sub-section.

CHAPTER IV
PROSECUTION WING

15. Appointment of Prosecution Director.

(1) The Lokpal may, by notification, constitute a prosecution wing and appoint a prosecution Director and such other officers and employees to assist the prosecution Director for the purpose of prosecution of public servants in relation to any complaint by the Lokpal under this Act.

(2) The prosecution Director shall, after having been so directed by the Lokpal, file a complaint before the Special Court, and take all necessary steps in respect of the prosecution of public servants in relation to any offence punishable under the Prevention of Corruption Act, 1988. (49 of 1988)

CHAPTER V
EXPENSES OF INSTITUTION OF LOKPAL TO BE CHARGED ON CONSOLIDATED FUND OF INDIA

16. Expenses of Lokpal to be charged on Consolidated Fund of India.

The expenses of the Lokpal, including all salaries, allowances and pensions payable to or in respect of the Chairperson, members or secretary or other officers or staff of the Lokpal, shall be charged on the Consolidated

Fund of India and any fees or other moneys taken by the Lokpal shall form part of that Fund.

CHAPTER VI

JURISDICTION IN RESPECT OF INQUIRY

17. Jurisdiction of Lokpal.

(1) Subject to the other provisions of this Act, the Lokpal shall inquire into any matter involved in, or arising from, or connected with, any allegation of corruption by a public servant made in a complaint in respect of the following, namely:–

(a) any person who is or has been a Minister of the Union other than the Prime Minister;

(b) any person who is or has been a Member of either House of Parliament;

(c) any Group 'A' officer or equivalent or above, when serving or who has served, in connection with the affairs of the Union;

(d) any chairperson or member or officer equivalent to Group 'A' officer referred to in clause (c) or equivalent or above in any body or Board or corporation or authority or company or society or autonomous body (by whatever name called) established or constituted under an Act of Parliament or wholly or partly financed by the Central Government or controlled by it;

(e) any director, manager, secretary or other officer of every other society or association of persons or trust (whether registered under any law for the time being in force or not) wholly or partly financed by the Government or in receipt of any sums under the Foreign Contribution (Regulation) Act, 1976 or any donation from the public: (49 of 1976)

Provided that the Lokpal shall not inquire into any matter involved in, or arising from, or connected with, any such allegation of corruption against any Member of either House of Parliament in respect of anything said or a vote given by him in Parliament or any committee thereof covered under the provisions contained in clause (2) of article 105 of the

Constitution. (45 of 1988)

(2) The Lokpal may inquire into any act or conduct of any person other than those referred to in sub-section (1), if such person is associated with the allegation of corruption under the Prevention of Corruption Act, 1988.

(3) No matter in respect of which a complaint has been made to the Lokpal under this Act, shall be referred for inquiry under the Commissions of Inquiry Act, 1952. (60 of 1952)

18. Matters pending before any court or committee or authority before inquiry before Lokpal not to be affected.

In case any matter or proceeding related to allegation of corruption under the Prevention of Corruption Act, 1988 has been pending before any court or committee of either House of Parliament or before any other authority prior to commencement of this Act or prior to commencement of any inquiry after the commencement of this Act, such matter or proceeding shall be continued before such court, committee or authority. (49 of 1988)

Explanation– For the removal of doubts, it is herby declared that continuance of such matter or proceeding before any court or committee of either House of Parliament or before any other authority, except for such matters as are protected under clause (2) of article 105 of the Constitution or are pending before a court, shall not affect the power of the Lokpal to inquire into such matter under this Act.

19. Constitution of benches of Lokpal.

(1) Subject to the provisions of this Act, –

(a) the jurisdiction of the Lokpal may be exercised by benches thereof;

(b) a bench may be constituted by the Chairperson with two or more Members as the Chairperson may deem fit;

(c) every bench shall ordinarily consist of at least one Judicial Member;

(d) where a bench consists of the Chairperson, such bench shall be presided over by the Chairperson;

(e) where a bench consists of a Judicial Member, and a non-Judicial Member, not being the Chairperson, such bench shall be presided over by the Judicial Member;

(f) the benches of the Lokpal shall ordinarily sit at New Delhi and at such other places as the Lokpal may, by regulations, specify.

(2) The Lokpal shall notify the areas in relation to which each bench of the Lokpal may exercise jurisdiction.

(3) Notwithstanding anything contained in sub-section (2), the Chairperson shall have the power to constitute or reconstitute benches from time to time.

(4) If at any stage of the hearing of any case or matter it appears to the Chairperson or a Member that the case or matter is of such a nature that it ought to be heard by a bench consisting of three or more Members, the case or matter may be transferred by the Chairperson or, as the case may be, referred to him for transfer, to such bench as the Chairperson may deem fit.

20. Distribution of business amongst Benches

Where benches are constituted, the Chairperson may, from time to time, by notification, make provisions as to the distribution of the business of the Lokpal amongst the benches and also provide for the matters which may be dealt with by each bench.

21. Power of Chairperson to transfer cases

On an application for transfer made by the complainant or the public servant, the Chairperson, after giving an opportunity of being heard to the complainant or the public servant, as the case may be, may transfer any case pending before one bench for disposal to any other bench.

22. Decision to be by majority.

If the Members of a bench consisting of two Members differ in opinion on any point, they shall state the point or points on which they differ, and make a reference to the Chairperson who shall either hear the point or points himself or refer the case for hearing on such point or points by one or more of the other Members of the Lokpal and such point or points shall be decided according to the opinion of the majority of the Members of the Lokpal who have heard the case, including those who first heard it.

CHAPTER VII
PROCEDURE IN RESPECT OF INQUIRY AND INVESTIGATION

23. Provisions relating to complaints and inquiry and investigation.

(1) The Lokpal, on receipt of a complaint, may either make preliminary inquiry or direct its Investigation Wing, to make a preliminary investigation to ascertain whether there exists a prima facie case for proceeding in the matter.

(2) Every preliminary inquiry or preliminary investigation referred to in sub-section (1) shall ordinarily be completed within a period of thirty days and for reasons to be recorded in writing, within a further period of three months from the date of receipt of the complaint.

(3) Upon completion of the preliminary investigation, the investigating authority shall submit its report to the Lokpal.

(4) Before the Lokpal comes to the conclusion in the course of a preliminary inquiry and after submission of a report referred to in sub-section (3) that a prima facie is made out against the public servant pursuant to such a preliminary inquiry, the Lokpal shall afford the public servant an opportunity to be heard consistent with principles of natural justice.

(5) Where the Lokpal, after receiving the report of the investigating authority pursuant to a preliminary investigation or conclusion of the preliminary inquiries as referred to in sub-section (1) is satisfied that no prima facie case is made out for proceeding further in the matter, the complaint shall be closed and the decision thereon be communicated to the complainant and the public servant.

(6) Where the Lokpal is of the opinion that prima facie case is made out and refers the matter for investigation, upon completion of such investigation and before filing the charge sheet, the public servant against whom such investigation is being conducted shall be given an opportunity to be heard consistent with the principles of natural justice.

(7) Every inquiry conducted by the Lokpal, upon being

satisfied that a prima facie case is made out, shall be open to the public provided that in exceptional circumstances and for reasons to be recorded in writing by the Lokpal, such inquiry may be conducted in camera.

(8) In case the Lokpal proceeds to inquire into the complaint, it shall hold such inquiry as expeditiously as possible and complete the inquiry within a period of six months from the date of receipt of the complaint which, for reasons to be recorded in writing, may be extended by a further period of six months.

(9) The public servant against whom an inquiry is being conducted under sub-section (8) shall be given an opportunity to be heard consistent with the principles of natural justice.

(10) Where in a case the Lokpal is of the opinion and reason to be recorded in writing that it is not in the interest of justice to either hold a preliminary inquiry or preliminary investigation, it may refer the matter for investigation.

(11)Upon completion of such investigation but before filing a charge sheet, the investigating authority shall place the records in its possession along with it prima facie conclusion before the Lokpal who shall before directing that a charge sheet be filed afford the public servant concerned an opportunity to be heard consistent with the principles of natural justice.

(12)If the Lokpal proposes to inquire into a complaint, it may, at any stage,–

(a) pass appropriate orders for safe custody of the documents relevant to the inquiry as it deems fit; and

(b) forward a copy of the complaint to the public servant concerned

24. Persons likely to be prejudicially affected to be heard.

If, at any stage of the proceeding, the Lokpal–

(a) considers it necessary to inquire into the conduct of any person other than the prospective accused; or

(b) is of opinion that the reputation of any person other than a accused is likely to be prejudicially affected by the inquiry, the Lokpal shall give to that person a reasonable opportunity of being heard in the inquiry and to produce evidence in his defence, consistent with the principles of natural justice:

Provided that nothing in this section shall apply where the credibility of a witness is being impeached.

25. Lokpal may require any public servant or any other person to furnish information, etc.

(1) Subject to the provisions of this Act, for the purpose of any inquiry or investigation, the Lokpal or the investigating authority, as the case may be, may require any public servant or any other person who, in its opinion, is able to furnish information or produce documents relevant to such inquiry or investigation, to furnish any such information or produce any such document.

26. Previous sanction not necessary for investigation and initiating prosecution by Lokpal in certain cases.

(1) No sanction or permission or authorisation shall be required by the Lokpal or its Investigation Wing under section 6A of the Delhi Special Police Establishment Act, 1946 (25 of 1946), or section 197 of the Code of Criminal Procedure, 1973 (2 of 1974) or section 19 of the Prevention of Corruption Act, 1988 (49 of 1988) for the purpose of making inquiry by the Lokpal or investigation by its Investigation Wing into any complaint against any public servant or for filing of any complaint in respect thereof before the Special Court under this Act.

(2) A Special Court may, notwithstanding anything contained in section 6A of the Delhi Special Police Establishment Act, 1946 (25 of 1946), or section 197 of the Code of Criminal Procedure, 1973 (2 of 1974) or section 19 of the Prevention of Corruption Act, 1988 (49 of 1988), on a complaint filed by the Lokpal or any officer authorised by it in this behalf, take cognizance of offence committed by any public servant.

(3) Nothing contained in sub-sections (1) and (2) shall apply in respect of the persons holding the office in pursuance of the provisions of the Constitution and in respect of which a procedure for removal of such person has been specified therein.

(4) The provisions contained in sub-sections (1), (2) and (3) shall be without prejudice to the generality of the provisions contained in article 311 and sub-clause (c) of clause (3) of article 320 of the Constitution.

27. Action on inquiry in relation to public servants not being minsters or Members of Parliament.

(1) Where after the conclusion of the inquiry or investigation, the findings of the Lokpal disclose the commission of an offence under the Prevention of Corruption Act, 1988 (49 of 1988) by a public servant referred to in clause (c) or clause (d) of sub-section (1) of section 17, the Lokpal may–

(a) file a case in the Special Court and send a copy of the report together with its findings to the competent authority;

(b) recommend to the competent authority the initiation of discliplinary proceedings under the rules of disciplinary proceedings applicable to such public servant;

(c) provide a copy of the report to the public servant or his representative;

(2) The competent authority shall, within a period of thirty days of the receipt of recommendation under clause (b) of sub-section (1), initiate disciplinary proceedings against the delinquent public servant accused of committing offence under the Prevention of Corruption Act, 1988 (49 of 1988) and forward its comments on the report, including the action taken or proposed to be taken thereon, to the Lokpal ordinarily within six months of initation of such disciplinary proceedings.

28. Action on inquiry against public servant being ministers or Members of Parliament.

(1) (1) Where after the conclusion of the inquiry or investigation, the findings of the Lokpal disclose the commission of an offence under the Prevention of Corruption Act, 1988 (49 of 1988) by a public servant referred to in clause (a) or clause (b) of sub-section (1) of section 17, the Lokpal may file a case in the Special Court and shall send a copy

of the report together with its findings to the competent authority;

(2) The Speaker, in the case of the Minister or a Member of the House of the People, and the Chairman of the Council of States, in the case of a Member of that Council shall, as soon as may be, after the receipt of report under sub-section (1), cause the same to be laid before the House of the People or the Council of States, as the case may be, while it is in session, and if the House of the People or the Council of States, as the case may be, is not in session, within a period of one week from the reassembly of the said House or the Council, as the case may be.

(3) The competent authority shall examine the report forwarded to it under sub-section (1) and communicate to the Lokpal, within a period of ninety days from the date of receipt of the report, the action taken or proposed to be taken on the basis of the report.

Explanation.– In computing the period of ninety days referred to in this sub-section, any period during which Parliament or, as the case may be, either House of Parliament, is not in session, shall be excluded.

CHAPTER VIII
POWERS OF LOKPAL

29. Search and seizure.

(1) If the Lokpal has reason to believe that any document which, in its opinion, shall be useful for, or relevant to, any investigation or inquiry under this Act, are secreted in any place, it may authorise any officer of Investigation Wing, to search for and to seize such documents.

(2) If the Lokpal is satisfied that any document seized under sub-section (1) would be evidence for the purpose of any investigation or inquiry under this Act and that it would be necessary to retain the document in its custody or in the custody of such officer as may be authorised, it may so retain or direct such officer authorised to retain such document till the completion of such investigation or inquiry:

Provided that where any document is required to be returned, the Lokpal or the authorised officer may return the same after retaining copies of such document duly authenticated.

(3) The provisions of the Code of Criminal Procedure, 1973 relating to searches shall, so far as may be, apply to searches under this section subject to the modification that sub-section (5) of section 165 of the said Code shall have effect as if for the word "Magistrate", wherever it occurs therein, the words "Lokpal or any officer authorised by it" were substituted. (2 of 1974)

30. Lokpal to have powers of civil court in certain cases.

(1) Subject to the provisions of this section, for the purpose of any inquiry, the Lokpal shall have all the powers of a civil court, under the Code of Civil Procedure, 1908, (5 of 1988) while trying a suit in respect of the following matters, namely:–

(i) summoning and enforcing the attendance of any person and examining him on oath;

(ii) requiring the discovery and production of any document;

(iii) receiving evidence on affidavits;

(iv) requisitioning any public record or copy thereof from any court or office;

(v) issuing commissions for the examination of witnesses or documents:

Provided that such commission, in case of a witness, shall be issued only where the witness, in the opinion of the Lokpal, is not in a position to attend the proceeding before the Lokpal; and

(vi) such other matters as may be prescribed.

(2) Any proceeding before the Lokpal shall be deemed to be a judicial proceeding within the meaning of section 193 of the Indian Penal Code. (45 of 1960)

Explanation.– For the purposes of this section, "public servant" shall have the same meaning as is in section 21 of the Indian Penal Code.

31. Power to punish for contempt.

The Lokpal shall have, and exercise, jurisdiction, powers and authority in respect of contempt of itself as the High Court has and may exercise such power or authority, for this purpose under the provisions of the Contempt of Courts Act, 1971, (70 of 1971) which shall have effect subject to the modification that–

(a) any reference therein to a High Court shall be construed as including a reference to the Lokpal;

(b) any reference to the Advocate General in section 15 of the said Act shall be construed as a reference to such law officer as the Lokpal may specify in this behalf:

Provided that such matters shall be heard by a Special Bench consisting of five Members constituted by the Chairperson.

32. Power of Lokpal to utilise services of officers of Central or State Government.

(1) The Lokpal may, for the purpose of conducting any inquiry, utilise the services of any officer or investigation agency of the Central Government or any State Government, as the case may be.

(2) For the purpose of investigating into any matter pertaining to the inquiry, any officer or agency whose services are utilised under sub-section (2) may, subject to the direction and control of the Lokpal,–

(a) summon and enforce the attendance of any person and examine him;

(b) require the discovery and production of any document; and

(c) requisition any public record or copy thereof from any office.

(3) The officer or agency whose services are utilised under sub-section (2) shall investigate into any matter pertaining to the inquiry and submit a report thereon to the Lokpal within such period as may be specified by the Lokpal in this behalf.

33. Provisional attachment of assets.

(1) Where the Lokpal or any investigation officer authorised by it in this behalf, has reason to believe, the reason for such belief to be be recorded in writing, on the basis of material in his possession, that–

(a) any person is in possession of any proceeds of corruption;

(b) such person is accused of having committed an offence relating to corruption; and

(c) such proceeds of offence are likely to be concealed, transferred or dealt with in any manner which may result in frustrating any proceedings relating to confiscation of such proceeds of offence, he may, by order in writing, provisionally attach such property for a period not exceeding ninety days from the date of the order, in the manner provided in the Second Schedule to the Income-tax Act, 1961 and the Lokpal shall be deemed to be an officer under sub-rule (e) of rule 1 of that Schedule: (43 of 1961)

(2) The Lokpal shall, immediately after attachment under sub-section (1), forward a copy of the order, along with the material in his possession, referred to in that sub-section, to the Special Court, in a sealed envelope, in the manner as may be prescribed and such Court may extend the order of attachment and keep such material for such period as the Court may deem fit.

(3) Every order of attachment made under sub-section (1) shall cease to have effect after the expiry of the period specified in that sub-section or after the expiry of the period as directed by the Special Court under sub-section (2).

(4) Nothing in this section shall prevent the person interested in the enjoyment of the immovable property attached under sub-section (1) or sub-section (2), from such enjoyment.

Explanation.— For the purposes of this sub-section, "person interested", in relation to any immovable property, includes all persons claiming or entitled to claim any interest in the property.

34. Confirmation of attachment of assets.

(1) The Lokpal, when it provisionally attaches any property under sub-section (1) of section 33 shall, within a period of thirty days of such attachment, direct its prosecution wing to file an application stating the facts of such attachment before the Special Court and make a prayer for confirmation of attachment of the property till completion of the proceedings against the public servant in the Special Court.

(2) The Special Court may, if it is of the opinion that the property provisionally attached had been acquired through corrupt means, make an order for confirmation of attachment of such property till the completion of the proceedings against the public servant in the Special Court.

(3) If the public servant is subsequently acquitted of the charges framed against him, the property, subject to the orders of the Special Court, shall be restored to the concerned public servant along with benefits from such property as might have accrued during the period of attachment.

(4) If the public servant is subsequently convicted of the charges of corruption, the proceeds relatable to the offence under the Prevention of Corruption Act, 1988 shall be confiscated and vest in the Central Government free from any encumbrance or leasehold interest excluding any debt due to any bank or financial institution. **(49 of 1988)**

Explanation.– For the purposes of this sub-section, the expressions "bank", "debt" and "financial institution" shall have the meanings respectively assigned to them in clauses (d), (g) and (h) of section 2 of the Recovery of Debts Due to Banks and Financial Institutions Act, 1993. **(51 of 1993)**

35. Power of Lokpal to recommend transfer or suspension of public servant connected with allegation of corruption.

(1) Where the Lokpal, while making an inquiry into allegations of corruption, is prima facie satisfied, on the basis of evidence available, that-

(a) the continuance of the public servant referred to in clause (c) or clause (d) of sub-section (1) of section 17 in his post while conducting the inquiry is likely to affect such inquiry adversely; or

(b) the public servant referred to in clause (a) is likely to destroy or in any way tamper with the evidence or influence witnesses,

then, the Lokpal may recommend to the Central Government for transfer or suspension of such public servant from the post held by him till such period as may be specified in the order.

(2) The Central Government shall ordinarily accept the recommendation of the Lokpal made under sub-section (1), except for the reasons to be recorded in writing in a case where it is not feasible for administrative reasons.

36. Power of Lokpal to give directions to prevent destruction of records during inquiry.

The Lokpal may, in discharge of its functions under this Act, issue appropriate directions to a public servant entrusted with the preparation or custody of any document or record–

(a) to protect such document or record from destruction or damage; or

(b) to prevent the public servant from altering or secreting such document or record; or

(c) to prevent the public servant from transferring or alienating any assets allegedly acquired by him through corrupt means.

37. Power to delegate.

The Lokpal may, by general or special order in writing, and subject to such conditions and limitations as may be specified therein, direct that any administrative or financial power conferred on it may also be exercised or discharged by such of its Members or officers or employees as may be specified in the order.

CHAPTER IX
SPECIAL COURTS

38. Special Courts to be notified by Central Government.

(1) The Central Government shall constitute such number of Special Courts, as recommended by the Lokpal, to hear and decide the cases arising out of the Prevention of Corruption Act, 1988 or under this Act. (49 of 1988)

(2) The Special Courts constituted under sub-section (1) shall ensure completion of each trial within a period of one year from the date of filing of the case in the Court:

Provided that in case the trial cannot be completed within a period of one year, the Special Court shall record reasons therefor and complete the trial within a further period of not more than three months or such further periods not exceeding three months each, for reasons to be recorded in writing, before the end of each such three month period, but not exceeding a total period of two years.

39. Letter of request to a contracting State in certain cases.

(1) Notwithstanding anything contained in this Act or the Code of Criminal Procedure, 1973 (2 of 1974) if, in the course of an inquiry or investigation into an offence or other proceeding under this Act, an application is made to a Special Court by the Investigation Officer of the Lokpal that any evidence is required in connection with the inquiry or investigation into an offence or proceeding under this Act and he is of the opinion that such evidence may be available in any place in a contracting State, and the Special Court, on being satisfied that such evidence is required in connection with the inquiry or investigation into an offence or proceeding under this Act, may issue a letter of request to a court or an authority in the contracting State competent to deal with such request to—

(i) examine the facts and circumstances of the case;

(ii) take such steps as the Special Court may specify in such letter of request; and

(iii) forward all the evidence so taken or collected to the Special Court issuing such letter of request.

(2) The letter of request shall be transmitted in such manner as the Central Government may prescribe in this behalf.

(3) Every statement recorded or document or thing received under sub-section (1) shall be deemed to be evidence collected during the course of the inquiry or investigation.

CHAPTER X
COMPLAINTS AGAINST CHAIRPERSON, MEMBERS AND OFFICIALS OF LOKPAL

40. Complaints against Chairperson and Members not to be inquired by Lokpal.

(1) The Lokpal shall not inquire into any complaint made against the Chairperson or any Member.

(2) Any complaint against the Chairperson or Member shall be made by an application by the party aggrieved, to the President.

(3) The President shall, in case there exists a prima facie case

for bias or corruption, make a reference to the Chief Justice of India in such manner as may be prescribed for inquiring into the complaint against the Chairperson or Member.

(4) The President shall decide the action against the Chairperson or Member on the basis of the opinion of the Chief Justice of India and in case the President is satisfied on the basis of the said opinion that the Chairperson or the Member is biased or has indulged in corruption, the President shall, notwithstanding anything contained in sub-section (1) of section 8, remove such Chairperson or Member and also order for initiation of prosecution in case of allegation of corruption.

41. Complaints against officials of Lokpal.

(1) Every complaint of allegation of wrongdoing made against any officer or employee or investigation agency under or associated with the Lokpal for offence punishable under the Prevention of Corruption Act, 1988 (49 of 1988) shall be dealt with in accordance with the provisions of this section.

(2) The Lokpal shall complete the inquiry into the complaint or allegation made, within a period of thirty days from the date of its receipt.

(3) While making an inquiry into the complaint against any officer or employee of the Lokpal or agency engaged or associated with the Lokpal, if it is prima facie satisfied on the basis of evidence available, that–

(a) continuance of such officer or employee of the Lokpal or agency engaged or associated in his post while conducting the inquiry is likely to affect such inquiry adversely; or

(b) an officer or employee of the Lokpal or agency engaged or associated is likely to destroy or in any way tamper with the evidence or influence witnesses,

then, the Lokpal may, by order, suspend such officer or employee of the Lokpal or divest such agency engaged or associated with the Lokpal of all powers and responsibilities hereto before exercised by it.

(4) On the completion of the inquiry, if the Lokpal is satisfied that there is prima facie evidence of the commission of an

offence under the Prevention of Corruption Act, 1988 (49 of 1988) or of any wrongdoing, it shall, within a period of fifteen days of the completion of such inquiry, order to prosecute such officer or employee of the Lokpal or such officer, employee, agency engaged or associated with the Lokpal and initiate disciplinary proceedings against the official concerned:

Provided that no such order shall be passed without giving such officer or employee of the Lokpal or person, agency engaged or associated, a reasonable opportunity of being heard.

CHAPTER XI
ASSESSMENT OF LOSS AND RECOVERY THEREOF BY SPECIAL COURT

42. Assessment of loss and recovery thereof by Special Court.

If any public servant is convicted of an offence under the Prevention of Corruption Act, 1988 (45 of 1988) by the Special Court, notwithstanding and without prejudice to any law for the time being in force, it may make an assessment of loss, if any, caused to the public exchequer on account of the actions or decisions of such public servant not taken in good faith and for which he stands convicted, and may order recovery of such loss, if possible or quantifiable, from such public servant so convicted:

Provided that if the Special Court, for reasons to be recorded in writing, comes to the conclusion that the loss caused was pursuant to a conspiracy with the beneficiary or beneficiaries of actions or decisions of the public servant so convicted, then such loss may, if assessed and quantifiable under this section, may also be recovered from such beneficiary or beneficiaries proportionately.

CHAPTER XII
FINANCE, ACCOUNTS AND AUDIT

43. Budget.

The Lokpal shall prepare, in such form and at such time in each financial year as may be prescribed, its budget for the next financial year, showing the estimated receipts and expenditure of the Lokpal and forward the same to the Central Government for information.

44. Grants by Central Government.

The Central Government may, after due appropriation made by Parliament by law in this behalf, make to the Lokpal grants of such sums of money as are required to be paid for the salaries and allowances payable to the Chairperson and other Members and the administrative expenses, including the salaries and allowances and pension payable to or in respect of officers and other employees of the Lokpal.

45. Annual statement of accounts.

(1) The Lokpal shall maintain proper accounts and other relevant records and prepare an annual statement of accounts in such form as may be prescribed by the Central Government in consultation with the Comptroller and Auditor-General of India.

(2) The accounts of the Lokpal shall be audited by the Comptroller and Auditor-General of India at such intervals as may be specified by him.

(3) The Comptroller and Auditor-General of India or any person appointed by him in connection with the audit of the accounts of the Lokpal under this Act shall have the same rights, privileges and authority in connection with such audit, as the Comptroller and Auditor-General of India generally has, in connection with the audit of the Government accounts and, in particular, shall have the right to demand the production of books, accounts, connected vouchers and other documents and papers and to inspect any of the offices of the Lokpal.

(4) The accounts of the Lokpal, as certified by Comptroller and Auditor-General of India or any other person appointed by him in this behalf, together with the audit report thereon, shall be forwarded annually to the Central Government and the Central Government shall cause the same to be laid before each House of Parliament.

46. Furnishing of returns, etc., to Central Government.

(1) The Lokpal shall furnish to the Central Government, at such time and in such form and manner as may be prescribed or as the Central Government may request, such returns and statements and such particulars in regard to any matter under the jurisdiction of the Lokpal, as the

Central Government may, from time to time, require.

(2) The Lokpal shall prepare, once every year, in such form and at such time as may be prescribed, an annual report, giving a summary of its activities during the previous year and copies of the report shall be forwarded to the Central Government.

(3) A copy of the report received under sub-section (2) shall be laid by the Central Government, as soon as may be after it is received, before each House of Parliament.

CHAPTER XIII
DECLARATION OF ASSETS

47. Declaration of assets.

(1) Every public servant shall make a declaration of his assets and liabilities in the manner as provided by or under this Act.

(2) A public servant shall, within a period of thirty days from the date on which he makes and subscribes an oath or affirmation to enter upon his office, furnish to the competent authority the information relating to—

(a) the assets of which he, his spouse and his dependent children are, jointly or severally, owners or beneficiaries;

(b) his liabilities and that of his spouse and his dependent children.

(3) A public servant holding his office as such, at the time of the commencement of this Act, shall furnish information relating to such assets and liabilities, as referred to in sub-section (2) to the competent authority within thirty days of the coming into force of this Act.

(4) Every public servant shall file with the competent authority, on or before the 31st July of every year, an annual return of such assets and liabilities, as referred to in sub-section (2), as on the 31st March of that year.

(5) The information under sub-section (2) or sub-section (3) and annual return under sub-section (4) shall be furnished to the competent authority in such form and in such manner as may be prescribed.

(6) The competent authority in respect of each office or Department shall ensure that all such statements are

published on the website of such officer or Department by 31st August of that year.

Explanation.– For the purposes of this section, "dependent children" means sons and daughters who have no separate means of earning and are wholly dependent on the public servant for their livelihood.

48. Presumption as to acquisition of assets by corrupt means in certain cases.

If any public servant wilfully or for reasons which are not justifiable, fails to–

(a) to declare his assets; or

(b) gives misleading information in respect of such assets and is found to be in possession of assets not disclosed or in respect of which misleading information was furnished,

then such assets shall, unless otherwise proved, be presumed to belong to the public servant and shall be presumed to be assets acquired by corrupt means:

Provided that the competent authority may condone or exempt the public servant from furnishing information in respect of assets not exceeding such minimum value as may be prescribed.

CHAPTER XIV
CITIZENS' CHARTER

49. Citizens' charter.

(1) Every,–

(a) Ministry or Department or office of the Central Government or any body or Board or corporation or authority or company or society or autonomous body (by whatever name called) established or constituted or incorporated under an Act of Parliament or wholly or partly financed by the Central Government or controlled by it; and

(b) every other society or association of persons or trust (whether registered or not) wholly or partly financed by the Government or in receipt of any sums under the Foreign Contribution (Regulation) Act or any donation from public,

shall prepare and publish a charter to be known as Citizens' Charter within a period of one year from the commencement of this Act.

(2) The Citizens' Charter referred to in sub-section (1) shall specify to the citizens the commitments of,—
   (a) the Ministry or Department or office of the Central Government or any body or Board or corporation or authority or company or society or autonomous body or other society or association of persons or trust referred to in that sub-section;
   (b) the officer responsible for meeting such commitment; and
   (c) the time within which such commitment shall be complied with along with other relevant details relating to public delivery of services or fulfilment of its objectives.

(3) Every Ministry or Department or office of the Central Government or any body or Board or corporation or authority or company or society or autonomous body or other society or association of persons or trust referred to in sub-section (1) shall designate an officer to be called the Public Grievance Redressal Officer to whom any aggrieved person may file a complaint for non-compliance of the Citizens' Charter:

(4) Every Ministry or Department or office of the Central Government or any body or Board or corporation or authority or company or society or autonomous body or other society or association of persons or trust shall appoint at least one Public Grievance Redressal Officer in each district where it has an office.

(5) Every Ministry or Department or office of the Central Government or any body or Board or corporation or authority or company or society or autonomous body or other society or association of persons or trust referred to in sub-section (1) shall review and revise its Citizens' Charter at least once in a year.

CHAPTER XV
OFFENCES AND PENALTIES

50. Prosecution for false complaint and payment of compensation, etc., to public servant.

(1) Notwithstanding anything contained in this Act, whoever makes any false and frivolous or vexatious complaint

under this Act shall, on conviction, be punished with imprisonment for a term which shall not be less than two years but which may extend to five years and with fine which shall not be less than twenty-five thousand rupees but which may extend to two lakh rupees.

(2) No Court, except a Special Court, shall take cognizance of an offence under sub section (1).

(3) No Special Court shall take cognizance of an offence under sub-section (1) except on a complaint made by a person against whom the false, frivolous or vexatious complaint was made.

(4) The prosecution in relation to an offence under sub-section (1) shall be conducted by the public prosecutor and all expenses connected with such prosecution shall be borne by the Central Government.

(5) In case of conviction of a person [being an individual or society or association of persons or trust (whether registered or not)], for having made a false complaint under this Act, such person shall be liable to pay compensation to the public servant against whom he made the false complaint in addition to the legal expenses for contesting the case by such public servant, as the Special Court may determine.

51. False complaint made by society or association of persons or trust.

(1) Where any offence under section 50 has been committed by any society or association of persons or trust (whether registered or not), every person who, at the time the offence was committed, was directly in charge of, and was responsible to, the society or association of persons or trust, for the conduct of the business or affairs or activities of the society or association of persons or trust as well as such society or association of persons or trust shall be deemed to be guilty of the offence and shall be liable to be proceeded against and punished accordingly:

Provided that nothing contained in this sub-section shall render any such person liable to any punishment provided in this Act, if he proves that the offence was committed without his knowledge or that he had exercised all due diligence to prevent the commission of such offence.

(2) Notwithstanding anything contained in sub-section (1), where an offence under this Act has been committed by a society or association of persons or trust (whether registered or not) and it is proved that the offence has been committed with the consent or connivance of, or is attributable to any neglect on the part of, any director, manager, secretary or other officer of such society or association of persons or trust, such director, manager, secretary or other officer shall also be deemed to be guilty of that offence and shall be liable to be proceeded against and punished accordingly.

CHAPTER XVI
MISCELLANEOUS

52. Protection of action taken in good faith by any public servant.

No suit, prosecution or other legal proceedings under this Act shall lie against any public servant, in respect of anything which is done in good faith or intended to be done in the discharge of his official functions or in exercise of his powers.

53. Protection of action taken in good faith by others.

No suit, prosecution or other legal proceedings shall lie against the Lokpal or against any officer, employee, agency or any person, in respect of anything which is done in good faith or intended to be done under this Act.

54. Members, officers and employees of Lokpal to be public servants.

The Chairperson, Members, officers and other employees of the Lokpal shall be deemed, when acting or purporting to act in pursuance of any of the provisions of this Act, to be public servants within the meaning of section 21 of the Indian Penal Code. **(45 of 1860)**

55. Bar of Jurisdiction.

No civil court shall have jurisdiction in respect of any matter which the Lokpal is empowered by or under this Act to determine.

56. Act to have overriding effect.

The provisions of this Act shall have effect notwithstanding anything inconsistent therewith contained in any enactment other than this Act or in any instrument having effect by virtue of any enactment other than this Act.

57. Provision of this Act to be in addition of other laws.

The provisions of this Act shall be in addition to, and not in derogation of, any other law for the time being in force.

58. Amendment of certain enactments.

The enactments specified in the Second Schedule shall be amended in the manner specified therein.

59. Power to make rules.

(1) The Central Government may, by notification in the Official Gazette, make rules to carry out the provisions of this Act.

(2) In particular, and without prejudice to the generality of the foregoing power, such rules may provide for all or any of the following matters, namely: –

(a) the term of the search committee, fee and allowances payable to its members and the manner of selection of panel of names under sub-section (5) of section 4;

(b) the procedure of inquiry into misbehaviour for removal of the Chairperson or any other Member under sub-section (1) of section 8;

(c) the post or posts in respect of which the appointment shall be made after consultation with the Union Public Service Commission under the proviso to sub-section (1) of section 11;

(d) other matters for which the Lokpal shall have the powers of a civil court under clause (vi) of sub-section (1) of section 30;

(e) the manner of sending the order of attachment along with the material to the Special Court under sub-section (2) of section 33;

(f) the manner of transmitting the letter of request under sub-section (2) of section 39;

(g) the manner of making reference to the Chief Justice of India under sub-section (3) of section 40;

(h) the form and the time for preparing in each financial year the budget for the next financial year, showing the estimated receipts and expenditure of the Lokpal under section 43;

(i) the form for maintaining the accounts and other relevant records and the form of annual statement of accounts under sub-section (1) of section 45;

(j) the form and manner and the time for preparing the returns and statements along with particulars under sub-section (1) of section 46;

(k) the form and the time for preparing an annual report giving a summary of its activities during the previous year under sub-section (2) of section 46;

(l) the form of annual return to be filed by a public servant under sub-section (5) of section 47;

(m) the minimum value for which the competent authority may condone or exempt a public servant from furnishing information in respect of assets under the proviso to section 48;

(n) any other matter which is to be or may be prescribed.

60. Power of Lokpal to make regulations.

(1) Subject to the provisions of this Act and the rules made thereunder, the Lokpal may, by notification in the Official Gazette, make regulations to carry out the provisions of this Act.

(2) In particular, and without prejudice to the generality of the foregoing power, such regulations may provide for all or any of the following matters, namely:—

(a) the conditions of service of the secretary and other officers and staff of the Lokpal and the matters which in so far as they relate to salaries, allowances, leave or pensions, require the approval of the President under sub-section (2) of section 11;

(b) the place of sittings of benches of the Lokpal under clause (f) of sub-section (1) of section 19;

(c) the manner for displaying on the website of the Lokpal, the status of all complaints pending or disposed of along with records and evidence with reference thereto under sub-section (13) of section 23;

(d) the manner and procedure of conducting an inquiry or investigation under sub-section (15) of section 23;

(e) any other matter which is required to be, or may be, specified under this Act.

61. Laying of rules and regulations.

Every rule and regulation made under this Act shall be laid, as soon as may be after it is made, before each House of Parliament, while it is in session, for a total period of thirty days which may be comprised in one session or in two or more successive sessions, and if, before the expiry of the session immediately following the session or the successive sessions aforesaid, both Houses agree in making any modification in the rule or regulation, or both Houses agree that the rule or regulation should not be made, the rule or regulation shall thereafter have effect only in such modified form or be of no effect, as the case may be; so, however, that any such modification or annulment shall be without prejudice to the validity of anything previously done under that rule or regulation.

62. Power to remove difficulties.

(1) If any difficulty arises in giving effect to the provisions of this Act, the Central Government may, by order, published in the Official Gazette, make such provisions not inconsistent with the provisions of this Act, as may appear to be necessary for removing the difficulty:

Provided that no such order shall be made under this section after the expiry of a period of two years from the commencement of this Act.

(2) Every order made under this section shall be laid, as soon as may be after it is made, before each House of Parliament.

11

Team Anna's Jan Lokpal Bill

An act to create effective anti-corruption and grievance redressal systems at centre so that effective deterrent is created against corruption and to provide effective protection to whistleblowers.

1. **Short title and commencement:-**
   (1) This Act may be called the Jan Lokpal Act, 2010.
   (2) It shall come into force on the one hundred and twentieth day of its enactment.
2. **Definitions:-** In this Act, unless the context otherwise requires,-
   (1) "Action" means any action taken by a public servant in the discharge of his functions as such public servant and includes decision, recommendation or finding or in any other manner and includes willful failure or omission to act and all other expressions relating to such action shall be construed accordingly;
   (2) "Allegation" in relation to a public servant includes any affirmation that such public servant-
      (a) has indulged in misconduct, if he is a government servant;
      (b) has indulged in corruption
   (3) "complaint" includes any grievance or allegation or a request by whistleblower for protection and appropriate action.
   (4) "corruption" includes anything made punishable under Chapter IX of the Indian Penal Code or under the Prevention of Corruption Act, 1988;
   Provided that if any person obtains any benefit from the government by violating any laws or rules, that person along with the public servants who directly or indirectly helped that person obtain those benefits, shall be deemed

to have indulged in corruption.

(5) "Government" or "Central Government" means Government of India.

(6) "Government Servant" means any person who is or was any time appointed to a civil service or post in connection with the affairs of the Central Government or High Courts or Supreme Court either on deputation or permanent or temporary or on contractual employment but would not include the judges.

(7) "grievance" means a claim by a person that he sustained injustice or undue hardship in consequence of mal-administration;

(8) "Lokpal" means
   a. Benches constituted under this Act and performing their functions as laid down under various provisions of this Act; or
   b. Any officer or employee, exercising its powers and carrying out its functions and responsibilities, in the manner and to the extent, assigned to it under this Act, or under various rules, regulations or orders made under various provisions of this Act.
   c. For all other purposes, the Chairperson and members acting collectively as a body;

(9) "Mal-administration" means action taken or purporting to have been taken in the exercise of administrative function in any case where,-
   a. such action or the administrative procedure or practice governing such action is unreasonable, unjust, oppressive or improperly discriminatory; or
   b. there has been willful negligence or undue delay in taking such action or the administrative procedure or practice governing such action involves undue delay;

(9A) "Minor penalty" and Major penalty" shall mean the same as defined in CCS Conduct Rules.

(10) "Misconduct" means misconduct as defined in relevant Conduct Rules and which has vigilance angle.

(11) "public authority" means any authority or body or institution of self- government established or constituted–
   a. by or under the Constitution;

b. by any other law made by Parliament;
c. by notification issued or order made by the Government, and includes any body owned, controlled or substantially financed by the Government;

(12) "Public servant" means a person who is or was at any time,-
(a) the Prime Minister;
(b) a Minister;
(c) a Member of Parliament;
(d) Judges of High Courts and Supreme Courts;
(e) a Government servant;
(f) the Chairman or Vice-Chairman (by whatever name called) or a member of a local authority in the control of the Central Government or a statutory body or corporation established by or under any law of the Parliament of India, including a co-operative society, or a Government Company within the meaning of section 617 of the Companies Act, 1956 and members of any Committee or Board, statutory or non-statutory, constituted by the Government;
(g) includes all those who are declared as "public servants" in section 2(c) of Prevention of Corruption Act 1988.
(h) Such other authorities as the Central Government may, by notification, from time to time, specify;

(13) "Vigilance angle" includes –
(a) All acts of corruption
(b) Gross or willful negligence; recklessness in decision making; blatant violations of systems and procedures; exercise of discretion in excess, where no ostensible/public interest is evident; failure to keep the controlling authority/superiors informed in time
(c) Failure/delay in taking action, if under law the government servant ought to do so, against subordinates on complaints of corruption or dereliction of duties or abuse of office by the subordinates
(d) Indulging in discrimination through one's conduct, directly or indirectly.
(e) Victimizing Whistle Blowers
(f) Any undue/unjustified delay in the disposal of a case,

perceived after considering all relevant factors, would reinforce a conclusion as to the presence of vigilance angle in a case.

(g) Make or undertake an unfair investigation or enquiry either to unduly help those guilty of corruption or incriminate the innocent.

(h) Any other matter as notified from time to time by the Lokpal

(14) "Whistleblower" is any person, who faces the threat of

(a) professional harm, including but not limited to illegitimate transfer, denial of promotion, denial of appropriate perquisites, departmental proceedings, discrimination or

(b) physical harm, or

(c) is actually subjected to such harm;

because of either making a complaint to the Lokpal under this Act, or for filing an application under the Right to Information Act, 2005 or by any other legal action aimed at preventing or exposing corruption or mal-governance.

3. **Establishment of the institution of Lokpal and appointment of Lokpal:**

(1) There shall be an institution known as Lokpal which shall consist of one Chairperson and ten members along with its officers and employees.

(2) The Chairperson and members of Lokpal shall be selected in such manner as laid down in this Act.

(3) A person appointed as Chairperson or member of Lokpal shall, before entering upon his office, make and subscribe before the President, an oath or affirmation in the form as prescribed.

(4) The Government shall appoint the Chairperson and members of the first Lokpal and set up the institution with all its logistics and assets within six months of enactment of this Act.

(5) The Government shall fill up a vacancy of the Chairperson or a member caused due to

a) Retirement, 3 months before the member or the Chairperson retires.

b) Any other unforeseen reason, within a month of such vacancy arising.

CHAIRPERSON AND MEMBERS OF LOKPAL

4. **The Chairperson and members of Lokpal not to have held certain offices-**

The Chairperson and members of Lokpal shall not be serving member of either the Parliament or the Legislature of any State and shall not hold any office or trust of profit (other than the office as Chairperson or member) or carry on any business or practice any profession and accordingly, before he enters upon his office, a person appointed as the Chairperson or member of Lokpal shall-

(i) if he holds any office of trust or profit, resign from such office; or

(ii) if he is carrying on any business, sever his connection with the conduct and management of such business; or

(iii) if he is practicing any profession, suspend practice of such profession.

(iv) If he is associated directly or indirectly with any other activity, which is likely cause conflict of interest in the performance of his duties in Lokpal, he should suspend his association with that activity.

Provided that if even after the suspension, the earlier association of that person with such activity is likely to adversely affect his performance at Lokpal, that person shall not be appointed as a member or Chairperson of Lokpal.

5. **Term of office and other conditions of service of Lokpal–**

(1) A person appointed as the Chairperson or member of Lokpal shall hold office for a term of five years from the date on which he enters upon his office or upto the age of 70 years, whichever is earlier;

Provided further that.-

(a) the Chairperson or member of Lokpal may, by writing under his hand addressed to the President, resign his office;

(b) the Chairperson or member may be removed from office in the manner provided in this Act.

(2) There shall be paid to the Chairperson and each member

every month a salary equal to that of the Chief Justice of India and that of the judge of the Supreme Court respectively;

(3) The allowances and pension payable to and other conditions of service of the Chairperson or a member shall be such as may be prescribed;

Provided that the allowances and pension payable to and other conditions of service of the Chairperson or members shall not be varied to his disadvantage after his appointment.

(4) The administrative expenses of the office of the Lokpal including all salaries, allowances and pensions payable to or in respect of persons serving in that office, shall be charged on the Consolidated Fund of India.

(5) There shall be a separate fund by the name of "Lokpal fund" in which penalties/fines imposed by the Lokpal shall be deposited and in which 10% of the loss of Public Money recovered under section 19 of this Act shall also be deposited by the Government. Disposal of such fund shall be completely at the discretion of the Lokpal and such fund shall be used only for enhancement/upgradation/extension of the infrastructure of Lokpal.

(6) The Chairperson and members of Lokpal shall not be eligible for appointment to any position in Government of India or Government of any state or any such body which is funded by any of the governments or for contesting elections to Parliament, state legislatures or local bodies, if he has ever held the position of the Chairperson or a member for any period after demitting their office. A member could be appointed as a chairperson, provided that the total tenure both as member and as chairperson would not exceed five years and no member or chairperson would be eligible for reappointment or extension after completion of a five year term.

6. **Appointment of the Chairperson and members:**

1. The Chairperson and members shall be appointed by the President on the recommendation of a selection committee.
2. The following shall not be eligible to become Chairperson or Member of Lokpal:
   (a) Any person, who is not a citizen of India
   (b) Any person, who was ever chargesheeted for any

offence under IPC or PC Act or any other Act or was ever penalized under CCS Conduct Rules.

(c) Any person, who is less than 40 years in age.

3. At least four members of Lokpal shall have legal background. Not more than two members, including Chairman, shall be former civil servants.

   Explanation: "Legal Background" means that the person should have held a judicial office in the territory of India for at least ten years or has been an advocate in High Court or Supreme Court for at least fifteen years.

4. The members and Chairperson should have unimpeachable integrity and should have demonstrated their resolve to fight corruption in the past.

5. A selection committee consisting of the following shall be set up:

   a. The Vice President of India
   b. Speaker of Lok Sabha
   c. Two senior most judges of Supreme Court
   d. Two senior most Chief Justices of High Courts.
   e. Retired army personnel who are five star Generals.
   f. Chairperson of National Human Rights Commission
   g. Comptroller and Auditor General of India
   h. Chief Election Commissioner
   i. After the first set of selection process, the outgoing members and Chairperson of Lokpal.

6. The Vice President shall act as the Chairperson of the selection committee.

7. The following selection process shall be followed:

   a. Recommendations shall be invited through open advertisements in prescribed format.
   b. Each person recommending shall be expected to justify the selection of his candidate giving examples from the past achievements of the candidate.
   c. The list of candidates along with their recommendations received in the format mentioned above shall be displayed on a website.
   d. Each member of the selection committee, on the basis of the above material, shall recommend such number

of names as there are vacancies.

e. This list shall be displayed on the website.

f. Public feedback shall be invited on the shortlisted names by putting these names on the website.

g. The selection committee may decide to use any means to collect more information about the background and past achievements of the shortlisted candidates.

h. All the material obtained so far about the candidates shall be made available to each member of the selection committee in advance. The members shall make their own assessment of each candidate.

i. The selection committee shall meet and discuss the material so received about each candidate. The final selections for the Chairperson and members shall be made preferably through consensus.

Provided that if three or more members, for reasons to be recorded in writing, object to the selection of any member, he shall not be selected.

j. All meetings of selection committee shall be video recorded and shall be made public.

8. The Prime Minister shall recommend the names finalized by the selection committee to the President immediately, who shall order such appointments within a month of receipt of the same.

9. If any of the members of the selection committee retires while a selection process is going on, that member will continue on the selection committee till the end of that process.

7. Removal of Chairperson or members-

(1) The Chairperson or any member shall not be removed from his office except by an order of the President on one or more of the following grounds:

a. Proved misbehavior

b. Professional, mental or physical incapacity

c. Insolvency

d. Being charged of an offence which involves moral turpitude

e. Engaging while holding such office, in any paid employment

f. Acquiring such financial interests or other interests, which are likely to affect his functions as member or Chairperson prejudicially.
g. Being guided by considerations extraneous to the merits of the case under his consideration with a view to favoring someone or implicating someone through any act of omission or commission.
h. Unduly influencing or attempting to influence any government functionary.
i. Committing any act of omission or commission which is punishable under Prevention of Corruption Act or is a misconduct.
j. If a member or the Chairperson in any way, concerned or interested in any contract or agreement made by or on behalf of any public authority in the Government of India or Government of any state or participates in any way in the profit thereof or in any benefit or emolument arising there from otherwise than as a member and in common with the other members of an incorporated company, he shall be deemed to be guilty of misbehavior.

(3) The following process shall be followed in respect of petitions for the removal of any member or Chairperson of Lokpal:

(a) Any person may move a petition before the Supreme Court seeking removal of one or more of the members or Chairperson of Lokpal, alleging one or more of the grounds for removal and providing evidence for the same.

(b) The Supreme Court will hear the matter on receipt of such petition and may take one or more of the following steps:

(i) order an investigation by a Special Investigation Team appointed by the Supreme Court, if a prima facie case is made out and if the matter cannot be judged based on affidavits of the parties. The Special Investigation Team shall submit its report within three months.

(ii) Pending investigations by a Special Investigation

Team under sub-clause (i), order withdrawal of a part or complete work from that member.

(iii) dismiss the petition if no case is made out

(iv) if the grounds are proved, recommend to the President for removal of the said member or Chairperson

(v) direct registration and investigation of cases with appropriate agencies, if there is a prima facie case of commission of an offence punishable under the Prevention of Corruption Act or any other law.

(d) The bench shall be constituted by a panel of five seniormost judges of the Supreme Court.

(e) The Supreme Court shall not dismiss such petitions in liminae.

(f) If the Supreme Court concludes that the petition has been made with mischievous or malafide motives, the Court may order imposition of fine or imprisonment upto one year against the complainant.

(g) On receipt of a recommendation from the Supreme Court under clause (b)(iv) supra, the Prime Minister shall immediately recommend the removal of the member(s) or Chairperson of Lokpal to the President, who shall order the removal of the said member(s) or Chairperson within a month of receipt of the same.

POWERS AND FUNCTIONS OF LOKPAL

8. **Functions of Lokpal:**

(1) the Lokpal shall be responsible for receiving:

(a) Complaints where there are allegations of acts of omission or commission punishable under the Prevention of Corruption Act

(b) Complaints where there are allegations of misconduct by a government servant,

(c) Grievances

(d) Complaints from whistleblowers

(e) Complaints against the staff of Lokpal

(1A)It shall be the prime duty of Lokpal to ensure the integrity of its own staff and employees, whether temporary or otherwise. Lokpal shall be competent and empowered to take all actions to ensure that.

(2) The Lokpal, after getting such enquiries and investigations done as it deems fit, may take one or more of the following actions:

a. Close the case, if prima facie, the complaint is not made out, or

b. Initiate prosecution against public servants as well as those private entities, which are parties to the act

c. Recommend imposition of appropriate penalties under the relevant Conduct Rules
Provided that if a government servant is finally convicted under the Prevention of Corruption Act, the penalty of dismissal shall be recommended on such government servant.

d. Order cancellation or modification of a license or lease or permission or contract or agreement, which was the subject matter of investigation.

e. Blacklist the concerned firm or company or contractor or any other entity involved in that act of corruption.

f. Issue appropriate directions to appropriate authorities for redressal of grievance as per provisions of this Act.

g. Invoke its powers under this Act if its orders are not duly complied with and ensure due compliance of its orders.

h. Take necessary action to provide protection to a whistleblower as per various provisions of this Act.

(3) Suo moto initiate appropriate action under this Act if any case, of the nature mentioned in clauses (a), (b), (c) or (d) of sub-section (1), comes to the knowledge of the Lokpal from any source.

(4) Issue such directions, as are necessary, from time to time, to appropriate authorities so as to make such changes in their work practices, administration or other systems so as to reduce the scope and possibility for corruption, misconduct, public grievances and whistleblower victimization.

(5) Orders made by Lokpal under sub-section (2)(c) of this section shall be binding on the government and the government shall implement it within a week of receipt of

that order.

(6) Section 19 of the Prevention of Corruption Act shall be deleted. Section 6A of Delhi Special Police Establishment Act shall not be applicable to the proceedings under this Act.

(7) Section 197 of CrPC shall not apply to any proceedings under this Act. All permissions, which need to be sought for initiating investigations or for initiating prosecutions under any Act shall be deemed to have been granted once Lokpal grants such permissions.

9. **Issue of Search Warrant, etc.-**

(1) Where, in consequence of information in his possession, the Lokpal

(a) has reason to believe that any person. –

(i) to whom a summon or notice under this Act, has, been or might be issued, will not or would not produce or cause to be produced any property, document or thing which will be necessary or useful for or relevant to any inquiry or other proceeding to be conducted by him;

(ii) is in possession of any money, bullion, jewellery or other valuable article or thing and such money, bullion, jewellery or other valuable article or thing represents either wholly or partly income or property which has not been disclosed to the authorities for the purpose of any law or rule in force which requires such disclosure to be made; or

(b) considers that the purposes of any inquiry or other proceedings to be conducted by him will be served by a general search or inspection, It may by a search warrant authorize any Police officer not below the rank of an Inspector of Police to conduct a search or carry out an inspection in accordance therewith and in particular to, -

(i) enter and search any building or place where he has reason to suspect that such property, document, money, bullion, jewellery or other valuable article or thing is kept;

(ii) search any person who is reasonably suspected of concealing about his person any article for which search should be made;

(iii) break open the lock of any door, box, locker safe, almirah or other receptacle for exercising the powers conferred by sub-clause (i) where the keys thereof are not available.

Seize any such property, document, money, bullion, jewellery or other valuable article or thing found as a result of such search;

(iv) place marks of identification on any property or document or make or cause to be made; extracts or copies therefrom; or

(v) make a note or an inventory of any such property, document, money, bullion, Jewellery or other valuable article or thing.

(2) The provisions of the Code of Criminal Procedure, 1973, relating to search and seizure shall apply, so far as may be, to searches and seizures under sub-section (1).

(3) A warrant issued under sub-section (1) shall for all purposes, be deemed to be a warrant issued by a court under section 93 of the Code of Criminal Procedure, 1973.

10. Evidence -

(1) Subject to the provisions of this section, for the purpose of any investigation (including the preliminary inquiry, if any, before such investigation) under this Act, the Lokpal may require any public servant or any other person who, in its opinion is able to furnish information or produce documents relevant to the investigation, to furnish any such information or produce any such document.

(2) For the purpose of any such investigation (including the preliminary inquiry) the Lokpal shall have all the powers of a civil court while trying a suit under the Code of Civil Procedure, 1908 , in respect of the following matters, namely:-

(a) Summoning and enforcing the attendance of any person and examining him on oath;

(b) Requiring the discovery and production of any document;

(c) Receiving evidence on affidavits;
(d) Requisitioning any public record or copy thereof from any court or office ;
(e) Issuing commissions for the examination of witnesses or documents ;
(f) ordering payment of compensatory cost in respect of a false or vexatious claim or defence;
(g) ordering cost for causing delay;
(h) Such other matters as may be prescribed.

(3) Any proceeding before the Lokpal shall be deemed to be a judicial proceeding with in the meaning of section 193 of the Indian Penal Code.

11. **Reports of Lokpal, etc.**

(1) The Chairperson of Lokpal shall present annually a consolidated report in prescribed format on its performance to the President.

(2) On receipt of the annual report, the President shall cause a copy thereof together with an explanatory memorandum to be laid before each House of the Parliament.

(3) The Lokpal shall publish every month on its website the list of cases disposed with brief details of each such case, outcome and action taken or proposed to be taken in that case. It shall also publish lists of all cases received by the Lokpal during the previous month, cases disposed and cases which are pending.

12. **Lokpal to be a deemed police officer:**

(1) For the purposes of section 36 of Criminal Procedure Code, the Chairperson, members of Lokpal and the officers in investigation wing of Lokpal shall be deemed to be police officers.

(2) While investigating any offence under Prevention of Corruption Act 1988, they shall be competent to investigate any offence under any other law in the same case.

13. **Powers in case of non-compliance of orders:**

(1) Each order of the Lokpal shall clearly specify the names of the officials who are required to execute that order, the manner in which it should be executed and the time period within which that order should be complied with.

(2) If the order is not complied with within the time or in the

manner directed, the Lokpal may decide to impose a fine on the officials responsible for the non-compliance of its orders.

(3) The Drawing and Disbursing Officer of that Department shall be directed to deduct such amount of fine as is clearly specified by the Lokpal in its order made in sub-section (2) from the salaries of the officers specified in the order.

Provided that no penalty shall be imposed without giving a reasonable opportunity of being heard.

Provided that if the Drawing and Disbursing Officer fails to deduct the salary as specified in the said order, he shall make himself liable for a similar penalty.

(4) In order to get its orders complied with, the Lokpal shall have, and exercise the same jurisdiction powers and authority in respect of contempt of itself as a High court has and may exercise, and, for this purpose, the provisions of the Contempt of Courts Act, 1971 (Central Act 70 of 1971) shall have the effect subject to the modification that the references therein to the High Court shall be construed as including a reference to the Lokpal.

13A.Special Judges under section 4 of Prevention of Corruption Act:

(1) On an annual basis, the Lokpal shall make an assessment of the number of Special Judges required under section 4 of the Prevention of Corruption Act 1988 in each area and the Government shall appoint such number of Judges within three months of the receipt of such recommendation.

Provided that the Lokpal shall recommend such number of Special Judges so that trial in each case under this Act is completed within a year.

(2) Before making any fresh appointments, the Government shall consult the Lokpal on the procedure to be followed in selection to ensure the integrity of the candidates selected. The Government shall implement such recommendations.

13B. Issue of Letter Rogatory: A bench of the Lokpal shall have powers to issue Letters Rogatory in any case pending with the Lokpal.

FUNCTIONING OF LOKPAL

14. Functioning of Lokpal:

(1) The Chairperson shall be responsible for the overall administration and supervision of the institution of Lokpal.

(2) All policy level decisions including formulation of regulations, developing internal systems for the functioning of Lokpal, assigning functions to various officials in Lokpal, delegation of powers to various functionaries in Lokpal etc shall be taken by the Chairperson and the members collectively as a body.

(3) The Chairperson shall have an annual meeting with the Prime Minister to assess the needs of Lokpal for finances and manpower. Lokpal shall be provided resources by the Government on the basis of outcome of this meeting.

(3A)The expenditure so decided shall be charged to Consolidated Fund of India.

(3B)Lokpal shall take all possible steps to ensure the integrity of its employees and integrity of all enquiries and investigations. For this purpose, it shall be competent to make rules, prescribe work norms and prescribe procedures for swift and effective punishment against inefficient and corrupt employees.

(4) Lokpal shall function in benches of three or more members. Benches shall be constituted randomly and cases shall be assigned to them randomly by computer. Each bench shall consist of at least one member with legal background.

(5) Such benches shall be responsible for

- (i) granting permission to initiate prosecution in cases against Joint Secretary and above.
- (ii) Hearing cases of complaints against its own staff.
- (iii) Such other orders as may be decided by Lokpal from time to time.

Provided that the full bench of Lokpal may lay down norms as to which category of cases will be dealt by the benches of members and which cases would be decided at the levels of Chief Vigilance officers or Vigilance Officers. The norms could be based on loss caused to the government and/or impact on public and/or the status of the accused.

(6) The Lokpal may decide to initiate investigations into any case suo motu.

(7) The decision to initiate investigation or prosecution against any member of the Cabinet shall be taken by full bench of Lokpal.

(8) Certain matters, as provided under this Act shall be dealt by the full bench of Lokpal, which shall consist of at least seven members.

(9) Minutes and records of meetings of Lokpal shall be made public.

15. Making a complaint to the Lokpal:

(1) Subject to the provisions of this Act, any person may make a complaint under this Act to the Lokpal.

Provided that in case of a grievance, if the person aggrieved is dead or for any reason, unable to act for himself, the complaint may be made or if it is already made may be continued by his legal representatives or by any other person who is authorized by him in writing in this behalf.

Provided further that a citizen may make a complaint to any office of Lokpal anywhere in the country. It shall be the duty of that office of Lokpal to transfer it to appropriate officer within Lokpal.

(2) A complaint could be on a plain paper but should contain all such details as prescribed by Lokpal.

(2A)After its annual report has been presented in the Parliament, the Comptroller and Auditor General of India shall forward all such cases, which constitute an allegation under this Act, to the Lokpal and Lokpal shall act on them as per provisions of this Act.

(3) On receipt of a complaint, the Lokpal shall decide whether it is an allegation or a grievance or a request for whistleblower protection or a mixture of two or more of these.

(4) Every complaint shall have to be compulsorily disposed of by the Lokpal.

Provided that no complaint shall be closed without giving an opportunity of hearing to the complainant.

16. Matters which may be investigated by the Lokpal–

Subject to the provisions of this Act, the Lokpal may investigate any action which is taken by or with the general or specific approval of a public servant where a complaint involving a grievance or an allegation is made in respect of such action. Provided that the Lokpal may also investigate such action suo moto or if it is referred to it by the government, if such action can be or could have been in his recorded opinion, subject of a grievance or an allegation.

17. **Matters not subject to investigation:-**

(1) The Lokpal shall not conduct any investigation under this Act in case of a grievance in respect of any action-

(i) if the complainant has or had, any remedy by way of appeal, revision, review or any other recourse before any authority provided in any other law and he has not availed of the same.

(ii) Taken by a judicial or quasi-judicial body, unless the complainant alleges malafides

(iii) If the substance of the entire grievance is pending before any court or quasi-judicial body of competent jurisdiction.

(iv) any grievance where there is inordinate and inexplicable delay in agitating it.

(2) Nothing in this Act shall be construed as authorising the Lokpal to investigate any action which is taken by or with the approval of the Presiding Officer of either House of Parliament.

(3) Nothing in this section shall bar Lokpal from entertaining a complaint making an allegation of misconduct or corruption or a complaint from a whistleblower seeking protection.

18. **Provisions relating to complaints and investigations-**

(i) (a) The Lokpal, on receipt of a complaint in the nature of an allegation or a grievance or a combination of the two, or in a case initiated on his own motion, may on perusing the documents, either decide to proceed to enquire or investigate into that complaint or decide, to make such preliminary inquiry before proceeding to enquire or investigate into such complaint or direct any other person to make such preliminary inquiry as it deems fit for ascertaining whether there exists a reasonable ground for conducting the investigation. The outcome of such preliminary enquiry, and if the complaint is being closed along with reasons for the same and all material collected during preliminary enquiry, shall be communicated to the complainant.

Provided that if any case is closed, all documents related thereto shall thereafter be treated as public. Every month, a list of all such cases shall be put on the website with reasons for closing a case. All material connected with such closed cases will be provided to anyone seeking it under Right to Information Act.

Provided further that no complaint of allegation shall be rejected on the basis of the motives or intention of the complainant.

Provided further that all hearings before Lokpal shall be video recorded and shall be available to any member of the public on payment of copying costs.

(b) The procedure for preliminary enquiry of a complaint shall be such as the Lokpal deems appropriate in the circumstances of the case and in particular, the Lokpal may, if it deems necessary to do so, call for the comments of the public servant concerned.

Provided that the preliminary enquiry should be completed and a decision taken whether to close a case or to proceed with investigations preferably within one month of receipt of any complaint, and positively within three months. Where the preliminary enquiry has not been completed within one month, reasons for the delay will be recorded in writing at the completion of the enquiry and made public.

(c) No anonymous complaint shall be entertained under this Act. The Complainant will have to reveal his identity to the Lokpal. However, if the complainant so desires, his identity shall be protected by Lokpal.

(ii) Where the Lokpal proposes, either directly or after making preliminary inquiry, to conduct any investigation under this Act, it.-

(a) may make such order as to the safe custody of documents relevant to the investigation, as it deems fit.

(b) at appropriate stage of investigations or in the end, it shall forward a copy of the complaint, its findings and copy of the material relied upon to the public servant concerned and the complainant,

(c) shall afford to such public servant and the complainant an opportunity to offer comments and be heard.

Provided that such hearing shall be held in public, except in rare circumstances, to be recorded in writing, where it is not in public interest and in the interest of justice to hold it in public, it will be held in camera.

(iii) The conduct of an investigation under this Act against a public servant in respect of any action shall not affect such action, or any power or duty of any other public servant to take further action with respect to any matter subject to the investigation.

(iv) If, during the course of a preliminary inquiry or investigation under this Act, the Lokpal is prima facie satisfied that the allegation or grievance in respect of any action is likely to be sustained either wholly or partly, it may, through an interim order, recommend the public authority to stay the implementation or enforcement of the decision or action complained against, or to take such mandatory or preventive action, on such terms and conditions, as it may specify in its order to prevent further harm from taking place. The public authority shall either comply with or reject the recommendations of Lokpal under this sub-section within 15 days of receipt of such an order. Lokpal, if it feels important, may approach appropriate High Court for seeking appropriate directions to the public authority.

(v) The Lokpal, either during the course of investigations, if it is satisfied that prosecution is likely to be initiated in that case, or at the end of the investigations at the time of initiating prosecution, shall make a list of moveable and immoveable assets of all the accused in that case and shall notify the same. No transfer of the same shall be permitted after such notification. In the event of final conviction, the trial court may, in addition to other measures, recover the loss determined under section 19 of this Act from this property,.

(vi) If during the course of investigation or enquiry into a complaint, the Lokpal feels that continuance of a public servant in that position could adversely affect the course of investigations or enquiry or that the said public servant is likely to destroy or tamper with the evidence or influence the witnesses, the Lokpal may issue appropriate recommendations including transfer of that public servant from that position or his suspension, if he is a government servant. The public authority shall either comply with or reject the recommendations of Lokpal under this sub-section within 15 days of receipt of such an order. Lokpal, if it feels important, may approach appropriate High Court for seeking appropriate directions to the public authority.

(vii) The Lokpal may, at any stage of inquiry or investigation under this Act, direct through an interim order, appropriate authorities to take such action as is necessary, pending inquiry or investigation.-

(a) to safeguard wastage or damage of public property or public revenue by the administrative acts of the public servant;

(b) to prevent further acts of misconduct by the public servant;

(c) to prevent the public servant from secreting the assets allegedly acquired by him by corrupt means;

The public authority shall either comply with or reject the recommendations of Lokpal under this sub-section within 15 days of receipt of such an order. Lokpal, if it feels important, may approach appropriate High Court for seeking appropriate directions to the public authority.

(viii) Where after investigation into a complaint, the Lokpal is satisfied that the complaint involving an allegation against the public servant, other than the Ministers, Members of Parliament and judges, is substantiated and that the public servant concerned should not continue to hold the post held by him, the Lokpal shall pass orders to that effect. In case of public servant being a Minister or a Member of Parliament, Lokpal shall make such recommendation to the President, who shall decide either to accept such recommendation or reject it within a month of its receipt. Provided that the provisions of this section shall not apply to the Prime Minister.

(ix) All records and information of Lokpal shall be public and shall be accessible under Right to Information Act, even at the stage of investigation or enquiry, unless the release of such information would adversely affect the process of enquiry or investigation.

RECOVERY OF LOSS TO THE GOVERNMENT AND PUNISHMENTS

19. **Recovery of loss to the Government:** When a person is convicted of an offence under the Prevention of Corruption Act 1988, then the trial court shall quantify the loss caused to the government and apportion that amount to various convicts from whom this money must be recovered as arrears of land revenue.

19A. **Punishments for offences:** For offences mentioned in Chapter III of the Prevention of Corruption Act, the proviso to section 2(4) of this Act and section 28A of this Act, the punishment shall not be less than two years of rigorous imprisonment and may extend upto life imprisonment.

Provided that if the accused is an officer of the rank of Joint Secretary or above or a Minister, a member or Chairperson of the Lokpal, the punishment shall not be less than ten years of imprisonment.

Provided further that if the offence is of the nature mentioned in the proviso to section 2(4) of this Act and if the beneficiary is a business entity, in addition to other punishments mentioned in this Act and under the Prevention of Corruption Act, a fine amounting to five times the loss caused to the public shall be recovered from the accused and the recovery may be done from the assets of the business entity and from the personal assets of all its Directors, if the assets of the accused are inadequate.

DEALING WITH COMPLAINTS AGAINST JUDGES OF HIGH COURTS OR SUPREME COURT

19B. **Receiving and disposing complaints against Judges of High Courts or Supreme Court:**

(1) Any complaint against any Judge of a High Court or Supreme Court shall be dealt only by the office of the

Chairperson of Lokpal.

(2) Each such complaint shall be subjected to a preliminary screening, which shall determine whether prima facie evidence exists of an offence under Prevention of Corruption Act. The screening shall be done by a member of Lokpal, who shall then present his findings to a full bench of Lokpal.

(3) A case shall not be registered without the approval of a full bench of Lokpal with majority of members of that bench being from legal background.

(4) Such case shall be investigated by a special team headed by an officer not below the rank of a Superintendent of Police.

(5) A decision whether to initiate prosecution shall be taken by a full bench of Lokpal with majority of members with legal background.

WHISTLEBLOWER PROTECTION

20. Protection of Whistleblower:

(1) A whistleblower may seek the protection of the Lokpal if he has been subjected to or threatened with, professional or physical victimization.

(2) On receiving such a complaint, Lokpal shall take following steps:

(a) Professional victimization: If after conducting appropriate enquiries, the Lokpal feels that there is a real threat to the whistleblower on account of having made an allegation under this Act, it shall, as soon as possible but not more than a month of receipt of such complaint, direct appropriate authorities to take such steps as directed by the Lokpal.

(b) If a whistleblower complains that he has been victimized professionally on account of making an allegation under this Act and the Lokpal, after conducting enquiries, is of the opinion that the whistleblower has been victimized for having made an allegation under this Act, it shall, as soon as possible but in not more than a month, direct appropriate authorities to take such steps as directed by the Lokpal.

Provided that for clause (a) the Lokpal may, but for clause

(b) the Lokpal shall, also issue orders imposing appropriate penalties under relevant Rules against the government servants who issued threats or caused victimization.

Provided further that no such penalties shall be imposed without giving an opportunity of being heard to the affected government servants.

(c) Threat of physical victimization: Lokpal shall conduct appropriate enquiries and if it feels that there is a real threat to the person and the threat is on account of that person having made an allegation under this Act or for having filed an RTI application to any public authority covered under this Act, then notwithstanding anything contained in any other law, the Lokpal shall pass appropriate orders, as soon as possible but in not more than a week, directing appropriate authorities, including police, to take such steps as directed by the Lokpal to provide adequate security to that person, to register criminal cases against those who are issuing threats and also to take all such steps necessary to mitigate circumstances leading to such threat.

Provided that if the threat is imminent, Lokpal may decide to act immediately, within a few hours to prevent physical assault on that person.

(d) If a person complains that he has already been physically assaulted on account of making an allegation under this Act and if Lokpal is satisfied after conducting enquiries that the person has been assaulted because of his having made an allegation under this Act or for filing an RTI application in any of the public authorities covered under this Act, then notwithstanding anything else contained in any other law, the Lokpal shall pass such orders, as soon as possible but in not more than 24 hours, directing the concerned authorities to take such steps as directed by the Lokpal to provide adequate security to that person, to register criminal cases and also to ensure that no further harm visits on that person.

(e) If the whistleblower has alleged an act punishable under Prevention of Corruption Act, then for cases under clause (c), Lokpal may and for cases under clause (d), the Lokpal shall, assign the allegations made by that person to a special team, put it on a fast track and complete investigations in that case in not more than a month.

(f) If the whistleblower has alleged an act punishable under any law other than the Prevention of Corruption Act, then for cases under clause (c), Lokpal may and for cases under clause (d), the Lokpal shall, direct the agency which has the powers to enforce that law to assign the allegations made by the whistleblower to a special team, put it on a fast track and complete investigations in that case in such time as directed by the Lokpal.

(g) Lokpal shall have the powers to issue directions to appropriate agencies in the cases covered under clause (f), monitor such investigations and if necessary, issue directions to that agency to do the investigations in the manner as directed by the Lokpal.

(h) Whistleblowers, who face threat of physical victimization or are actually assaulted may directly approach the Chairperson of Lokpal who shall meet them within 24 hours of their seeking such meeting and shall take appropriate action as per provisions of this Act.

(3) If any complainant requests that his identity should be kept secret, Lokpal shall ensure the same. Lokpal shall prescribe detailed procedures on how such complaints shall be dealt with.

(4) Lokpal shall Issue orders to the Public Authorities to make necessary changes in their policies and practices to prevent recurrence of victimization.

(5) Lokpal shall make appropriate rules for the receipt and disposal of complaints from whistleblowers.

GRIEVANCE REDRESSAL SYSTEMS

21. Citizens' Charters:

(1) Each public authority shall be responsible for ensuring the preparation and implementation of Citizens Charter, within a reasonable time, and not exceeding one year from

the coming into force of this Act.

(2) Every Citizens Charter shall enumerate the commitments of the respective public authority to the citizens, officer responsible for meeting each such commitment and the time limit with in which the commitment shall be met.

(3) Each public authority shall designate an official called Public Grievance Redressal Officer, whom a complainant should approach for any violation of the Citizens Charter.

Provided that a public authority shall appoint at least one Public Grievance Redressal Officer in each station, where they have an office.

Provided further that the Public Grievance Redressal Officer shall either be Head of that Department or an officer not more than one rank below him but if that station does not have a Head of Department in any station, the seniormost officer in that station shall be appointed as the Public Grievance Redressal Officer.

(4) Every public authority shall review and revise its Citizens Charter at least once every year through a process of public consultation to be held in the presence of Chief Vigilance Officer in that public authority.

(5) Lokpal may direct any public authority to make such changes in their citizens' charter as are mentioned in that order and that public authority shall make such changes within a week of receipt of such order.

Provided that such changes shall have to be approved by at least a three member bench of Lokpal.

Provided further than such changes should not increase the existing time limits or reduce the number of items in citizen's charter.

21A.Receipt and disposal of Grievances:

(1) The Chief Vigilance Officer of any public authority shall declare such number of Vigilance Officers, as it deems fit, to be known as Appellate Grievance Officers, to receive and dispose grievances related to that public authority.

(2) If a citizen fails to receive satisfactory redressal to his grievance within a month of making a complaint to Public Grievance Redressal Officer, can make a complaint to Appellate Grievance Officer.

Provided that if Appellate Grievance Officer feels that considering the gravity or urgency of the grievance, it is necessary to do so, he may decide to accept such grievance earlier also.

(3) If the complaint does not relate to an issue mentioned in Citizen's Charter of that public authority, the Appellate Grievance Officer, within a month of receipt of complaint, pass an order either rejecting the grievance or directing the public authority to redress the grievance in the manner and within such time, as is mentioned in the order.

Provided that no grievance shall be rejected without giving a reasonable opportunity of being heard to the complainant.

(4) A complaint to the Appellate Grievance Officer shall be deemed to have a vigilance angle if any of the following two conditions are satisfied:

- (i) for issues mentioned in citizen's charter, if a citizen fails to get satisfactory redressal from Public Grievance Redressal Officer.
- (ii) for issues other than those mentioned in citizen's charter, if the orders of Appellate Grievance Officer made under sub-section (3) of this section are violated.

(5) Each case, as mentioned in sub-section (4) of this section, shall be dealt in the following manner:

- (i) After giving a reasonable opportunity of being heard, the Appellate Grievance Officer shall pass an order fixing responsibility for failure to satisfactorily redress complainant's grievance in prescribed time and direct the Drawing and Disbursing Officer of that public authority to deduct from the salary of such officials, as mentioned in the order, such penalty amounts as are directed by Appellate Grievance Officer, which shall not be less than Rs 250 per day of delay calculated from the day the time limit mentioned in citizens' charter or the time limit specified in the order passed under sub-section (3) of this section, for redressing that grievance got over,
- (ii) Direct the Drawing and Disbursing Officer to compensate the complainant with such amounts as

are deducted from the salaries of the said officers.

(6) The Officers mentioned in the order made under clause (i) of sub-section (5) of this section shall be required to show cause that they acted in good faith and did not have corrupt motives. If they fail to do so, the Appellate Grievance Officer shall proceed to recommend penalties against the said officers under CCS Conduct Rules.

IMPOSITION OF MAJOR AND MINOR PENALTIES

21B. Allegations of misconduct shall be received and enquired by vigilance officers.

21C. Allegations of misconduct and public grievances with deemed vigilance angle under section 21A shall be dealt in the following manner:

(1) The vigilance officer shall conduct an enquiry into each such case within three months of its receipt and present its report to the Chief Vigilance Officer.

(2) Within a fortnight of receipt of report, the Chief Vigilance Officer shall constitute a three member bench of Deputy Chief Vigilance Officers other than the one who conducted enquiry at clause (1) above.

(3) The bench shall hold a summary hearing giving reasonable opportunity to the vigilance officer who conducted enquiry, the complainant and the officers accused.

(4) The bench shall hold hearings on day to day basis and pass an order either imposing one or more of the minor or major penalties on the accused government servants.

Provided that such orders shall be passed within a month of constitution of the bench.

Provided that such order shall be in the form of a recommendation to the appropriate appointing authority.

(5) An appeal shall lie against the order of the bench before the Chief Vigilance officer, who shall pass an order within a month of receipt of appeal, after giving reasonable opportunity to the accused, the complainant and the vigilance officer who conducted enquiries.

EMPLOYEES AND STAFF AND AUTHORITIES IN LOKPAL

22. Chief Vigilance Officer:

(1) There shall be a Chief Vigilance Officer in each public

authority to be selected and appointed by Lokpal.

(2) He shall not be from the same public authority.

(3) He shall be a person of impeccable integrity and ability to take proactive measures against corruption.

(4) He shall be responsible for accepting complaints against any public authority and shall transfer the complaints related to other public authorities within two days of receipt.

(5) He shall be responsible for carrying out all such responsibilities as assigned to him from time to time by Lokpal including dealing with complaints in the manner as laid down by Lokpal from time to time.

Provided that the complaints which require investigations under Prevention of Corruption Act 1988 shall be transferred to the Investigative wing of Lokpal.

Provided further that the complaints, other than grievances, against officers of the level of Joint Secretary or above shall not be dealt by the Chief Vigilance Officer and shall be transferred to the Lokpal, who shall set up a committee of Chief Vigilance Officers of three other public authorities to enquire into such complaint.

(6) All the grievances shall be received and disposed by Chief Vigilance Officer on behalf of Lokpal, if the citizen fails to get satisfactory redressal from Public Grievance Officer under section 21 of this Act.

(7) Such number of Vigilance Officers shall be appointed under the Chief Vigilance Officer as are decided by Lokpal from time to time.

(8) The Vigilance Officers and the Chief Vigilance Officer shall have powers to enquire and impose penalties under CCS Conduct Rules in such cases and as per such rules as laid down by the Lokpal from time to time.

23. Staff of Lokpal, etc.-

(1) There shall be such officers and employees as may be prescribed to assist the Lokpal in the discharge of their functions under this Act.

(2) The number and categories of officers and employees shall be decided by the Lokpal.

(3) The categories, recruitment and conditions of service of the officers and employees referred in sub-section (1) including

such special conditions or special pay as may be necessary for enabling them to act without fear in the discharge of their functions, shall be such as may be prescribed by Lokpal.

Provided that no official, whose integrity is in doubt, shall be considered for being posted in Lokpal.

Provided further that all officers and employees, who work in Lokpal on deputation or otherwise shall be eligible for the same terms and conditions as prescribed under this clause.

(4) Without prejudice to the provisions of sub-section (1), the Lokpal may for the purpose of conducting investigations under this Act utilize the services of.-

(a) any officer or investigating agency of the Central Government; or

(b) any officer or investigating agency of any other Government with the prior concurrence of that Government; or

(c) any person, including private persons, or any other agency.

(5) The officers and other employees referred to in sub-section (1) shall be under the administrative and disciplinary control of the Lokpal:

(6) Lokpal shall have the powers to choose its own officials. Lokpal may enlist officials on deputation from other government agencies for a fixed tenure or it may enlist officials on permanent basis from other government agencies or it may appoint people from outside on permanent basis or on a fixed tenure basis.

(7) The staff and officers shall be entitled to such pay scales and other allowances, which may be different and more than the ordinary pay scales in the Central Government, as are decided by the Lokpal from time to time, in consultation with the Prime Minister, so as to attract honest and efficient people to work in Lokpal.

(8) Lokpal shall be competent to increase or decrease its staff at various levels, within its overall budgetary constraints, depending upon its workload and keeping in mind the terms and conditions of the staff employed.

24. Repeal and savings–

(1) The Central Vigilance Commission Act shall stand repealed.

(2) Notwithstanding such repeal, any act or thing done under the said Act shall be deemed to have been done under this Act and may be continued and completed under the corresponding provisions of this Act.

(3) All enquiries and investigations and other disciplinary proceedings pending before the Central Vigilance Commission and which have not been disposed of, shall stand transferred to and be continued by the Lokpal as if they were commenced before him under this Act.

(4) Notwithstanding anything contained in any Act, the posts of the Secretary and other Officers and Employees of the Central Vigilance Commission are hereby abolished and they are hereby appointed as the Secretary and other officers and employees of the Lokpal. The salaries, allowances and other terms and conditions of services of the said Secretary, officers and other employees shall, until they are varied, be the same as to which they were entitled to immediately before the commencement of this Act.

(5) All vigilance administration under the control of all Departments of Central Government, Ministries of the Central Government, corporations established by or under any Central Act, Government companies, societies and local authorities owned or controlled by the Central Government shall stand transferred, alongwith its personnel, assets and liabilities to Lokpal for all purposes.

(6) The personnel working in vigilance wings of the agencies mentioned in sub-section (5) shall be deemed to be on deputation to Lokpal for a period of five years from the date they are transferred to Lokpal. However, Lokpal may decide to repatriate any one of them anytime.

(7) That Department from where any personnel have been transferred to Lokpal under sub-section (5), shall cease to have any control over the administration and functions of transferred personnel.

(8) Lokpal shall rotate the personnel and create vigilance wing of each department in such a way that no personnel from the same department get posted for vigilance functions in

the same department.

(9) No person shall be employed with Lokpal against whom any vigilance enquiry or any criminal case is pending at the time of being considered.

25. **Investigation Wing of Lokpal:**

(1) There shall be an investigation wing at Lokpal.

(2) Notwithstanding anything contained in section 17 of Prevention of Corruption Act, such officers of Investigation wing, upto the level as decided by Lokpal, shall have, in relation to the investigation and arrest of persons throughout India, in connection with investigation of complaints under this Act, all the powers, duties, privileges and liabilities which members of Delhi Special Police Establishment have in connection with the investigation of offences committed therein.

(3) That part of Delhi Special Police Establishment, in so far as it relates to investigation and prosecution of offences alleged to have been committed under the Prevention of Corruption Act, 1988, shall stand transferred, alongwith its employees, assets and liabilities to Lokpal for all purposes.

(4) That part of Delhi Special Police Establishment, which has been transferred under sub-section (3), shall form part of Investigation Wing of Lokpal.

(5) The Central Government shall cease to have any control over the transferred part and its personnel.

(6) The salaries, allowances and other terms and conditions of services of the personnel transferred under sub-section (3) shall be the same as to which they were entitled to immediately before the commencement of this Act.

(7) All cases which were being dealt by that part of Delhi Special Police Establishment, which has been transferred under sub-section (3), shall stand transferred to Lokpal.

(8) After completion of investigation in any case, the investigation wing shall present the case to an appropriate bench of Lokpal, which shall decide whether to grant permission for prosecution or not.

26. **Complaints against officers or employees of Lokpal:**

(1) Complaints against employees or officers of Lokpal shall be dealt with separately and as per provisions of this section.

(2) Such complaint could relate to an allegation of an offence punishable under Prevention of Corruption Act or a misconduct or a dishonest enquiry or investigation.

(3) As soon as such a complaint is received, the same shall be displayed on the website of Lokpal, alongwith the contents of the complaint.

Provided that if the complainant so desires, his identity shall be protected.

(4) Investigations into each such complaint shall be completed within a month of its receipt.

(5) In addition to examining the allegations against the said official, the allegations shall especially be examined against sections 107, 166, 167, 177, 182, 191, 192, 196, 199, 200, 201, 202, 204, 217, 218, 219, 463, 464, 468, 469, 470, 471, 474 of Indian Penal Code.

(6) If, during the course of investigations, it is felt that the charges are likely to be sustained, such officer shall be divested of all his responsibilities and powers and shall be placed under suspension.

(7) If after completion of enquiry or investigations, it is decided to prosecute that person under Prevention of Corruption Act, 1988 or he is held guilty of any misconduct or of conducting dishonest enquiry or investigations, then that person shall not work with Lokpal anymore. Lokpal shall either dismiss that person from the job, if that person is in the employment of Lokpal, or shall repatriate him, if he is on deputation, with a recommendation for his removal.

Provided that no order under this clause shall be passed without giving reasonable opportunity of being heard to the accused person.

Provided further that order under this clause shall be passed within 15 days of completion of investigations.

(8) A three member bench shall hear the cases of complaints against its staff and employees. However, for officers of the level of Chief Vigilance Officer or above, the hearings shall be done by full bench of Lokpal.

(9) Lokpal shall take all steps to ensure that all enquiries and investigations on complaints against its own staff and officials are conducted in most transparent and honest

manner.

27. Protection-

(1) No suit, prosecution, or other legal proceedings shall lie against the Chairperson or members or against any officer, employee, agency or person referred to in Section 14(4) in respect of anything which is in good faith done while acting or purporting to act in the discharge of his official duties under this Act.

(2) No proceedings of the Lokpal shall be held to be bad for want of form and except on the ground of jurisdiction, no proceedings or decision of the Lokpal shall be liable to be challenged, reviewed, quashed or called in question in any court of ordinary Civil Jurisdiction.

MISCELLANEOUS

28. Public Servants to submit property statements-

(1) Every public servant, other than those mentioned in Section 2(12)(a) to (c), shall within three months after the commencement of this Act and thereafter before the 30th June of every year submit to the head of that public authority, in the form prescribed by Lokpal, a statement of his assets and liabilities and those of the members of his family. Public servants mentioned in sections 2(12)(a) to (c) shall submit their returns in a format prescribed by the Lokpal, which shall include their sources of incomes, to the Lokpal with the aforesaid time lines.

(2) The Head of each public authority shall ensure that all such statements are put on the website by 31st August of that year.

(3) If no such statement is received by the Head of that public authority from any such public servant within the time specified in sub-section (1), the Head of that public authority shall direct the concerned public servant to do so immediately. If within next one month, the public servant concerned does not submit such statement, the Head shall stop the salary and allowances of that public servant till he submits such statement.

Explanation- In this section "family of a public servant" means the spouse and such children and parents of the public servant as are dependent on him.

(4) The Lokpal may initiate prosecution against such public servant under Section 176 IPC.

28A. Properties deemed to have been obtained through corrupt means:-

(1) If any property, moveable or immoveable, is subsequently found to be owned by the public servant or any of his family members, which had not been declared under this section by that public servant and which was acquired before filing of last return under this section, the same shall be deemed to have been obtained through corrupt means.

(2) If any property, moveable or immoveable, is subsequently found to be in possession of the public servant or any of his family members, which had not been declared under this section by that public servant, the same shall be deemed to be owned by that public servant and the same shall be deemed to have been acquired through corrupt means by that public servant, the onus of proving otherwise shall be on the public servant.

(3) The public servant shall be given an opportunity to explain, within 15 days,

(a) in the case of properties under sub-section (1) of this section, whether he had disclosed that property in any of the earlier years.

(b) in the case of properties under sub-section (2) of this section, to explain why these properties should not be deemed to be owned by the public servant.

(4) If public servant fails to provide satisfactory reply under sub-section (3) of this section with respect to some properties, Lokpal shall immediately confiscate all such properties.

(5) Transfer of those properties for which notices are issued under sub-section (3) of this section, shall be deemed to be null and void after the date of issue of such notices.

(6) Lokpal shall intimate such information to the Income Tax Department for appropriate action.

(7) Appeal against the orders of Lokpal shall lie in High Court of appropriate jurisdiction, which shall decide the matter within two months of filing of the appeal.

Provided that no appeal shall be entertained after expiry of 30 days from the date of order of Lokpal under sub-section (4).

(8) All properties confiscated under this section shall be auctioned to highest bidder. Half of the proceeds from the same shall be deposited by the Lokpal in Consolidated Fund of India. The balance amount could be used by Lokpal for its own administration.
Provided that if an appeal has been filed in any case, the auction shall not take place till the disposal of appeal.

28B.

(1) Within three months after the conclusion of any elections to the Parliament, the Lokpal shall compare the property statements filed by the candidates with Election Commission of India with their sources of income available with Income Tax Department. In such cases where assets are found to be more than known sources of income, it shall initiate appropriate proceedings.

(2) For an allegation against a Member of Parliament that he has taken a bribe for any conduct in Parliament, including voting in Parliament or raising question in Parliament or any other matter, a complaint could be made to the Speaker of Lok Sabha or the Chairperson of Rajya Sabha, depending upon the House to which that member belongs. Such complaints shall be dealt in the following manner:
   (a) The complaint shall be forwarded to the Ethics Committee within a month of its receipt.
   (b) The Ethics Committee shall, within a month, decide whether to.

29. Power to delegate and assign functions:

(1) Lokpal shall be competent to delegate its powers and assign functions to the officials working in Lokpal.

(2) All functions carried out and powers exercised by such officials shall be deemed to have been so done by the Lokpal.
Provided that the following functions shall be performed by the benches and cannot be delegated:
   (i) Granting permission to initiate prosecution in any case.
   (ii) Order for dismissal of any government servant under CCS Conduct Rules.
   (iii) Passing orders under section 10 on complaints against

officials and staff of Lokpal.

(iv) Pass orders in cases of complaints, other than grievances, against officers of the level of Joint Secretary and above.

30. **Time limits:**

(1) Preliminary enquiry under sub-section (1) of section 9 of this Act should be completed within a month of receipt of complaint.

Provided that the enquiry officer shall be liable for an explanation if the enquiry is not completed within this time limit.

(2) Investigation into any allegation shall be completed within six months, and in any case, not more than one year, from the date of receipt of complaint.

(3) Trial in any case filed by Lokpal should be completed within one year. Adjournments should be granted in rarest circumstances.

30A. **Transparency and application of Right to Information Act:**

(1) Lokpal shall make every effort to put every information on its website.

(2) A citizen would have a choice to make an appeal under section 19(3) of Right to Information Act, either with a member of Lokpal, so appointed for this purpose, or with the Central Information Commission. However, once having exercised that choice, he cannot go to the other authority for the same matter.

31. **Penalty for certain types of complaint-**

(1) Notwithstanding anything contained in this Act, if someone makes any complaint under this Act, which lacks any basis or evidence and is held by Lokpal to be meant only to harass certain authorities, Lokpal may impose such fines on that complainant as it deems fit.

Provided that no fine can be imposed without giving a reasonable opportunity of being heard.

Provided further that merely because a case could not be proved under this Act after investigation shall not be held against a complainant for the purposes of this section.

(2) Such fines shall be recoverable as dues under Land Revenue Act.

(3) A complaint or allegation once made under this Act shall not be allowed to be withdrawn.

31A. Preventive measures:

(1) Lokpal shall, at regular intervals, either study itself or cause to be studied the functioning of all public authorities falling within its jurisdiction and in consultation with respective public authority, issue such directions as it deems fit to prevent incidence of corruption in future.

(2) Lokpal shall also be responsible for creating awareness about this Act and involving general public in curbing corruption and maladministration.

31B. Reward Scheme:

(1) Lokpal shall encourage complainants from within and outside the government to report and fight against corruption by publicly recognizing such persons.

(2) Lokpal shall also prepare an appropriate scheme to give financial award to such complainants.

Provided that the total value of such reward shall not exceed 10% of the value of property confiscated or loss prevented.

32. Power to make Rules–

(1) The Government may, by notification in the Official Gazette, make rules for the purpose of carrying into effect the provisions of this Act.

Provided that such rules shall be made only in consultation and with the approval of Lokpal.

(2) In particular, and without prejudice to the generality of the foregoing provisions, such rules may provide for .-

(i) the allowance and pensions payable to and other conditions of service of the Chairperson and members of Lokpal;

(ii) the powers of a Civil Court which may be exercised by the Lokpal under clause (h) of sub-section (2) of section 11;

(2A)Lokpal shall also be competent to make its own rules for the proper functioning of Lokpal.

(i) the salary, allowances, recruitment and other conditions of service of the staff and employees of the Lokpal;

(iii) procedure for registration of cases at Lokpal and initiation of prosecution

(iv) any other matter for which rules have to be made are necessary under this Act.

(3) Any rule made under this Act may be made with retrospective effect and when such a rule is made the reasons for making the rule shall be specified in a Statement laid before both Houses of the Parliament.

(4) Lokpal shall strictly adhere to the time limits mentioned at various places in this Act. In order to achieve that, Lokpal shall lay down work norms for each level of functionaries and make an assessment of the additional number of functionaries and budget required in accordance with workload.

33. **Removal of difficulties-**

Notwithstanding anything contained in this Act, the President, in consultation with Lokpal or on request of Lokpal may, by order, make such provision -

(i) for bringing the provisions of this Act into effective operation;

(ii) for continuing the enquiries and investigations pending before the Central Vigilance Commission by the Lokpal.

34. **Power to make regulations:**

Lokpal shall have power to make its own regulations for the smooth functioning of the institution and to effectively implement various provisions of this Act.

35. **This Act shall override the provisions of all other laws.**

Selected Bibliography

Search Engines & Websites

www.google.com, www.yahoo.com, www.indiatimes.com, www.annahazare.org, www.wikipedia.org, www.indiaagainstcorruption.org

Newspapers & Magazines

Hindustan Times, Times of India, The Hindu, The Tribune, The Asian Age, The Indian Express, The Pioneer, India Today, Outlook, Organiser Weekly

TV News Channels

Aaj Tak, IBN-7, India TV, Live India, NDTV India, India News, STAR News, Zee News, DD News, BBC World, CNN IBN, Headlines Today, NDTV 24x7

Books

Hazare, Anna; Ganesh Pangare, Vasudha Lokur (1996). Adarsh Gaon Yojana: government participitation in a peoples program : ideal village project of the Government of Maharashtra. Hind Swaraj Trust.

Hazare, Anna. My Village – My Sacred Land.

Hazare, Anna (1997). Ralegaon Siddhi: a veritable transformation. Translated by B.S. Pendse. Ralegan Siddhi Pariwar Prakashan.